Entry into the American Labor Force

QUANTITATIVE STUDIES IN SOCIAL RELATIONS

Consulting Editor: Peter H. Rossi

UNIVERSITY OF MASSACHUSETTS
AMHERST, MASSACHUSETTS

Entry into the American Labor Force

Michael D. Ornstein

Department of Sociology and
Institute for Behavioral Research
York University
Downsview, Ontario, Canada

ACADEMIC PRESS   New York   San Francisco   London

A Subsidiary of Harcourt Brace Jovanovich, Publishers

ACADEMIC PRESS, INC.
111 Fifth Avenue, New York, New York 10003

United Kingdom Edition published by
ACADEMIC PRESS, INC. (LONDON) LTD.
24/28 Oval Road, London NW1

Library of Congress Cataloging in Publication Data

Ornstein, Michael D
    Entry into the American labor force.

    (Quantitative studies in social relations series)
    Bibliography: p.
    Includes index.
        1.   Labor and laboring classes—United States
2.   Occupational mobility—United States.
I.   Title.
HD8072.085 1976   331.1'1'0973   75-16876
ISBN 0–12–527950–7

Contents

Acknowledgments

This study of entry into the labor force is part of a larger research program carried out at the Johns Hopkins University from 1968 to 1973. The "Social Accounts Project" was originated by Professors James S. Coleman and Peter H. Rossi. It focused on the analysis of a set of life history data for Americans, the data that are used here.

I am indebted to Dr. Zahava Blum, who supervised the whole of the data gathering process; to Nancy Karweit of the Center for Social Organization of Schools and Aage B. Sørenson for organizing a data retrieval system for the complex longitudinal interviews; to John Kervin, Richard Conviser, Page Clark, and Charles Berry for their part in preparing the data; and to Shirley Sult, Joyce O'Keeffe, Jo-Anne DeGabriele, Helen Aron, Sylvia Ruddy, Pat Humenyk, Laura McPhail, and Jane Allain for typing manuscripts.

Peter H. Rossi supervised the preparation of the doctoral dissertation of which this monograph is a revision. He provided many valuable suggestions and a great deal of encouragement. I wish to thank James S. Coleman, Laura Morlock, and Gordon Darroch for their helpful criticisms. The shortcomings of this study are entirely mine.

The research could not have been carried out without the generous assistance of the Manpower Administration of the U.S. Department of Labor, which provided a grant (Number 91-24-71-01) for the specific analysis of entry into the labor force presented here. The entire project was supported by the Center for Social Organization of Schools at the Johns Hopkins University (Grant Number OEG-2-7-061610-0207). Neither of the granting agencies bears any responsibility for the conclusions reached in this monograph.

Introduction 1

The investigators in San José were left with the definite impression that chance has much to do with "landing" the first permanent job. For many a boy in the sample this first job had a decisive effect upon his subsequent occupational career, and the assignment of so dominating a role to mere chance presumably often has unfortunate results.[1]

Most youngsters (and their parents) approached the choice of a first job with no clear conception of where they were going; the great majority of first jobs were found in a very informal way, preponderantly through relatives and friends; the great majority of youngsters took the first jobs they found and did not make comparisons with any other job; their knowledge of the job before they took it was extremely meager and in most cases the job turned out to be a blind alley which did not lead to anything better.[2]

Three major generalizations sum up much of the research on factors affecting occupational careers. First, despite the net upward mobility which prevails in industrial societies, there is some tendency for men to inherit the occupational status levels of their fathers. Second, people are strongly influenced by the advice of significant others when they select jobs and choose occupational aspiration levels. Third, the general values which people hold are systematically related to their aspiration levels and to the kind of occupations they choose.[3]

For American men between the ages of 26 and 35, from nonfarm backgrounds, one third of the variation in the socioeconomic ranking of the first job is explained by their own educational attainment combined with the education and occupation of

[1] From Percy E. Davidson & H. Dewey Anderson. *Occupational mobility in an American community*. Palo Alto: Stanford University Press, 1937. P. 39.

[2] From Lloyd G. Reynolds. *The structure of labor markets*. New York: Harper, 1951. Pp. 127–128.

[3] From Richard L. Simpson & Ida Harper. Social origins, occupational advice, occupational values and work careers. *Social Forces*, March 1962, 40:264.

their fathers. Also, one third of the differences in the ranking of their later jobs can be attributed to the first job.[4]

Entry into the labor force marks a critical point in the lives of most Americans; it has no less important consequences for the nature of the social stratification process in the whole of the society. The personal impact of entering the labor force is not limited to finding a job and becoming a full-time worker, for it affects many other aspects of the way a person lives. It is one element of a transition into adulthood—individuals leave the families in which they were raised and form their own households, some move from the locale in which they grew up, everyone eventually leaves the relatively structured situation of a school or college to face an anarchic labor market. Until very recently, entry into the labor force exposed young American men to the military draft. The income from these first jobs makes young workers participants, though at very different levels, in a consumer culture.

To some extent, all men and women share a common experience as they enter the labor force. But entry also serves to separate men from women, whites from blacks and people of other races, the well educated from those with little schooling, the rich from the poor. For some Americans, entry into the labor force provides the opportunity to make use of their long years of education and training; for the nation's disadvantaged, it may mean no more than the chance to trade disinterested attendance in inferior schools for low-paying jobs. The amount of education with which individuals enter the labor force and the jobs they hold during the first years after entry are important determinants of the jobs they will hold and the income they will earn in the rest of their working days. A disproportionate amount of occupational mobility occurs in the first years of work experience, and young workers are much more likely to move from one region to another than are older workers.

Entry into the labor force marks two important divisions within the social stratification process. It separates each person's education from work experience, and it is the first point at which occupations can be traced from one generation to the next. The two variables defined by this

[4] Computed from Peter M. Blau & Otis Dudley Duncan, *The American occupational structure*. New York: Wiley, 1967. Chap. 5.

passage from school to work—the respondent's education and the ranking of his first job—are important elements in the models of the stratification process which have come to be developed recently. The critical relationships between the occupations of fathers and their sons, between an individual's first and later jobs, and between schooling and occupation first come to be defined at entry.

This study is a detailed examination of the way in which a sample of American men entered the labor force in the postwar period. In the sections that follow, we will argue that while the topic has attracted a great deal of attention from social scientists, a number of its most important features are quite poorly understood. The review of the research in this area is very selective and is intended only as a summary of the most important findings to date. A broad bibliographic review of empirical studies on entry, by Jeffrey Piker (1968), does exist. After presenting a critique of this work, we will go on to describe the survey data used in the analysis, the methodology employed, and the strategy of this investigation. Our discussion is limited to the experiences of men entering the labor force, since the sample survey includes interviews only with men.

PREVIOUS RESEARCH

The most common focus of research on entry has been on the perpetuation of inequalities in the family backgrounds of individuals and in their levels of educational attainment in the jobs held after entry. There is massive evidence to show that men from poorer backgrounds—as measured by their parents' educational attainments, occupations, or income— themselves obtain less schooling, experience more unemployment, have lower occupational aspirations, and find poorer jobs. This holds true whether the quality of the job is measured by gross occupational categories, with a prestige or socioeconomic scale, or in terms of income. As early as 1937, Davidson and Anderson in their Works Progress Administration assisted study of youth in San José reported that while chance seemed to play a large part in determining the kinds of jobs youth obtained, there were also important differences according to the level of skill of the individual. Survey research techniques have developed a great deal since this early work, as has our understanding of the occupational stratification process, but these advances have resulted in an elaboration of the first findings, rather than in any challenge to their validity.

The development of national sample surveys and of scales for ranking occupations, and the increasing use of multivariate regression and path analysis techniques have made it possible to describe entry into the labor force at the national level and to specify the roles and relative strengths of competing influences on this experience. The most ambitious of these studies, that of Blau and Duncan (1967:170), shows that about one-third of the variation in the quality of the first job, as measured using a socioeconomic scale of occupations, can be explained by the respondent's educational attainment together with the education and occupation of his father. Moreover, Blau and Duncan show that the respondent's education and his father's occupation directly influence the quality of his first job, but that the father's education has only an indirect effect, which is transmitted by the other two variables.

The Career Thresholds study (Parnes, Miljus, Spitz, and Associates 1970; Zeller, Shea, Kohen, and Meyer 1970; Kohen and Parnes 1971; Kohen and Andrisani 1973), based on a panel of about 5000 youths, shows that older, better educated individuals from more prosperous families know more about the labor market, have higher educational and occupational expectations, obtain more education, experience less unemployment, and get better jobs with higher pay. Beginning in 1959, the Bureau of Labor Statistics has included supplementary questions in its monthly labor force survey for October, in order to obtain information on the labor force status and jobs held by high school graduates and dropouts.[5] More recently, they have reported on the jobs of men with higher levels of education, too. Their surveys provide very accurate information on the extent of unemployment among young workers and on the occupations and industries (in gross categories) in which they obtain jobs. Strikingly higher unemployment rates are consistently found among high

[5] These surveys on the employment of high school graduates and dropouts have appeared in *Monthly Labor Review*, generally in one of the issues between May and September, and separately as Special Labor Force Reports of the Bureau of Labor Statistics. Each report contains a reprint of the article and, in addition, an explanatory note and supplementary tables. The reports include Cooper (1960), Perrella (1964), O'Boyle (1968), Hayghe (1972), and Michelotti (1974), which appear as Special Labor Force Reports 5, 14, 100, 145, and 168, respectively.

school dropouts. Unfortunately analysis of this potentially rich source of information about entry has so far been restricted to the computation of simple rates and distributions. A number of other, smaller scale studies have arrived at conclusions similar to the ones obtained by these larger efforts (see Piker 1968:20–31).

Individual characteristics do not exactly determine the levels of education with which men enter the labor force or the kinds of jobs they obtain subsequently; only about one-third of the variation in educational attainment can be explained by measures of family background (Duncan 1967:370), a proportion that rises to about 40% when a measure of intelligence is added (Duncan, Featherman, and Duncan 1972:Chap. 5). Nor do more elaborate models that include several measures of intelligence and of motivation have significantly greater predictive power (see Sewell, Haller, and Portes 1969; Sewell, Haller and Ohlendorf 1970; Duncan, Featherman, and Duncan 1972:Chap. 6; Porter, 1974). Family background and education account for about one-third of the variation in the socioeconomic rank of the first job, and in this case the addition of intelligence and motivation does little to reduce the uncertainty. Though the path analysis methods now coming into common use describe the interrelationships among the variables that describe the process of occupational achievement in a more detailed way than was previously possible, we have yet to see models that account for more than one-half of the variation in educational and occupational achievement.[6]

What are we to make of this? Jencks et al. (1972:227–228) argue that unexplained variation should simply be regarded as the effect of "luck," of factors beyond the control of any individual. To illustrate the effects of "luck," they note that the range of jobs available when a person is actually looking for a position may severely restrict his choice, and that the workers in some firms are eligible for overtime while those employed by others are not. From the viewpoint of the *individual* these are random events, but, in order to construct models that fully explain the occupational achievement process, they cannot be relegated to an unexplained residual category. To take another example, two individuals doing exactly the same job are likely to have different rates of pay, depending on the

[6] The first use of path models to describe the occupational stratification process is Duncan and Hodge (1963). A number of important examples are in Duncan (1966); the standard introduction is Land (1969).

firm in which they work—yet these differences are hardly inexplicable, even if the place where an individual finds work is largely determined by chance. So the unexplained variation can be attributed to these systemic factors and to characteristics of the individual that are inaccurately measured or that do not enter into the models. It is likely that some characteristics that are not clearly hierarchical or easily ranked, say meticulousness or presence of mind or even friendliness, have some influence on occupational achievement. The larger task we must face sometime is to add the structural variables into the models of individual behavior that now exist.

A second major set of findings concerns the impact of race. The results are predictable: Blacks and other minorities are "disadvantaged relative to whites, not only educationally, but also in respect to *all other career contingencies*" (Blau and Duncan 1967:209; emphasis added). They go on,

> In sum, Negroes are handicapped by having poorer parents, less education, and inferior early career experiences than whites. Yet even if these handicaps are statistically controlled by asking, in effect, what the achievement of non-whites would be if they had the same origins, the same education and the same first jobs as whites, their occupational chances are still consistently inferior to those of whites.

Numerous studies have described the nature of this institutional racism. Each stage in the stratification process not only perpetuates earlier disadvantages but adds of a new source of inequality; racism pervades the *process* as a whole.[7] The deficits attributable to race are not so large as the difference between the two ends of the educational distribution, but this is not to say that these racial differences are small.

The nature of racial differences in the values of entrants and the impact of these values on occupational outcomes is a more problematic issue. Parnes *et al.* (1970:179, 181) find that the occupational aspirations of blacks are higher than those of whites, when parental occupation and high school curriculum are (separately) held constant. Yet the later

---

[7] Among the most important sources on black–white educational and occupational differences are Duncan (1965), Hare (1965), Siegel (1965), Leiberson and Fuguitt (1967), and Duncan (1968).

achievement levels of whites no doubt will be considerably higher. Piker's survey of this area leads him to conclude that "the level of Negro youths' job preferences is variously found to be lower than, equal to, and higher than that of their white counterparts [1968:11]." Porter's (1974) comparison of the role of a number of psychological variables in black and white educational and early occupational achievement shows that there are fundamental differences in the patterns of relationships between the two races.

Many researchers have concentrated on aspects of the entry process itself, including the way in which entrants locate job openings, sources of information about the labor market, the extent of unemployment, job satisfaction, migration, and the impact of marital status. The single best source of this kind of information is the Career Thresholds study; Piker (1968:101–145) cites over 50 sources dealing with these issues. The material on specific aspects of the process of entry is less complete than that concerning the effects of class, race, and education, and because of its complexity cannot be so easily or coherently organized. But the directions of most of the relationships are reasonably predictable. For example, an examination of the methods used to locate the first job reveals that the proportion of job-seekers using friends and relatives to locate jobs diminishes with increasing education and that greater proportions of non-whites than of whites use informal connections to locate jobs (U.S. Department of Labor 1966:94). A number of studies show that entrants do not spend much time looking for the best available job but tend to select one of the first they find (see Lipset, Bendix, and Malm 1955; Simpson and Harper 1962; Sheppard and Belitsky 1966). Stigler (1962) argues that this makes sense, since the expected gain from locating additional job opportunities, beyond the first few, is relatively small, provided the variation in the quality of the alternative jobs is not too large.

Finally, we ask whether the entry process is important, whether it exerts any independent effects on later occupational achievement, effects that cannot be explained by such other antecedent variables as education or family background? The best answer, at present, is provided by Blau and Duncan, who find that the first job after entry does exert a considerable independent effect on later occupations, as well as playing an important role as a variable intervening between an individual's family background and his education and later attainment. Although the direct effect of the first job on later jobs is not as great as that of an individual's education, its direct effect is considerably larger than that of his *father's* education or occupation (See Blau and Duncan 1967:170).

Criticism

Perhaps the most fundamental difficulty with the research on entry into the labor force has been a lack of clarity as to the definition of entry. The point at which entry has occurred is taken to be self-evident. But it is not. Though the entry point may be clear-cut for the majority of young workers—who leave school for the last time and start the first of a series of jobs, never returning to school—some men join the armed forces and then return to school, others leave school for a year, to work, and then return to school for some years. Furthermore, if the respondent is asked to identify his own first job, he may forget a low-paying job that he held for just a short time and, instead, report his first "good" job or the first one that lasted for some time. So, a man who washed cars for 1 month after leaving school, before finding a job as a technician that he held for 5 years, might identify the second, longer job as his first job.

Blau and Duncan (1967:166–167) find that their "first job" variable suffers from these ambiguities in the definition of entry. Their question about the first job reads:

> Please think about the first full-time job you had after you left school. (Do not count part-time jobs or jobs during school vacation. Do not count military service). (a) How old were you when you began this job? (b) What kind of work were you doing? (c) What kind of business or industry was this? [p. 446].

Duncan, Featherman, and Duncan examine the responses to this item and conclude, from the relationships between the variables measuring the highest grade of school completed and age at entry, that sizable numbers of respondents either misreported one of the items or left school, took a full-time job, then returned to school. As evidence of the problem, they note that "something over a sixth of the men who reported having completed at least a year of graduate study, for example, also report that they had taken their first job before they reached the age of 19 [1972: 210]." The remedy suggested is to ask for "the first job after you first attended regular school." This change in the wording of the item no doubt will provide a more reliable variable; it is a sensible solution if a *single* measure of the level of entry is required, in order to develop a model of the whole occupational achievement process. But such a single variable cannot be sufficient to describe the mobility processes occurring as an individual enters the labor force.

The Career Thresholds study adopts a clearer definition of the first job; it is "the first job at which the respondent worked for two or more consecutive weeks after discontinuing regular school [Kohen and Andrisani 1973:138]." They survey men at the time of entry into the labor force, which virtually eliminates problems of recall, and their longitudinal data allow for the substitution of some other definition of entry, should the one above prove unsatisfactory. While more precise than Blau and Duncan's definition of entry, the Career Thresholds definition could result in men entering the labor force *more than once*, should they return to "regular school" after working for some period.

The problem of defining entry has important implications for the kind of data that can best be used to study entry into the labor force. Unless the researcher is prepared to provide his respondents with a precise description of how to identify their first jobs—which creates a further difficulty of tying the researcher to one definition and perhaps of increasing measurement error—longitudinal data are required. Ideally, the researcher should have available a listing of the respondent's work experiences, his school attendance, and his military service, which will make it possible to apply a set of criteria to the data, to identify the entry point. Whether some new definition will affect the results of the analysis is certainly not clear; it may be that Blau and Duncan's loose definition describes the entry point perfectly satisfactorily. However, we cannot know if this is the case until a more detailed study of entry is available.

A second implication of this problem of deciding when entry takes place, and a shortcoming of most of the existing research, is that entry must be seen as a *process*, rather than as a single point in time. The available literature has almost nothing to say about occupational mobility in the first years after an individual leaves school. Our understanding of educational mobility suffers from the same difficulty—although considerable numbers of entrants acquire some more schooling in the years after entry, we persist in assuming that educational attainment can also be defined as a single variable which is established at the point just before entry takes place. Thus, the lack of a temporal dimension in the conceptualization of the entry process restricts our understanding and tends to give most empirical analyses of entry a certain static quality. The cure is simple, but it depends on the availability of longitudinal data; the researcher must deal with a series of jobs over a period of time. Cross-sectional data simply cannot deal with early mobility processes.

In order to examine occupational, wage, and educational mobility in the period after entry, the analysis must be structured around the definition of entry chosen. The common technique of comparing individuals of the same age (as in much of the Bureau of Labor Statistics research) obscures the mobility that occurs in the first years of work, by lumping new entrants with individuals who have several years of work experience. At the age of 21, a high school dropout may have 5 years work experience, a college graduate could be looking for his first job after entry, while most professionals are still in college.

Much of the material on entry also suffers from a severe methodological shortcoming. Only a few of the most recent studies employ multivariate analysis, so most of the research consists of reports about bivariate relationships. Although multivariate methodology and causal modeling have developed rapidly in the past decade, simple tabular analysis so far continues to be applied to the two best current sources of material on entry into the labor force, the Career Thresholds panel data and the Bureau of Labor Statistics surveys. Nor have regression methods been used to attempt to disaggregate the differences between blacks and whites as they enter the labor force.

Multivariate analysis can also prove valuable in dealing with intervening variables in the entry process. Thus, it is well established that men with more education are more likely to use certain methods to locate jobs than are the less well educated. But what is *not* known is whether the method used to find a job has any impact on the quality of the job found—certainly the techniques of finding jobs will be of much more interest to researchers when it can be shown that they have some independent effects on occupational achievement. The simple remedy is to examine the relationship between the method and the job located, holding constant educational attainment, family background, and perhaps other variables.

A final limitation of the existing work on entry into the labor force concerns the consequences of entry. Although it is unlikely that the difficulties with their definition of entry have led Blau and Duncan to err substantially in estimating the long-term effects of the first job, we clearly can hope for a more precise measurement of its impact on later occupational achievement. More serious, though, is the absence of data on the connection between wages at entry and later in an individual's career—or on how mobility in the wage dimension might be related to mobility on some occupational scale. It is also possible that the relationships of race, family background, and education to wages will not be the same as for the socioeconomic rankings used in models to date. We should note that some longitudinal data on income do exist (as Featherman 1971), but they do not cover the entry period. Piker (1968) concludes his review of the literature on entry with these arguments:

> There has been almost a total absense of longitudinal studies of entry into the labor force. In most cases, research has consisted of a single snapshot the investigator had of a single point in a respondent's life, with the future relegated to anticipation by the respondent or inference by the researcher. Using such a method, it is difficult to provide a sense of process and transition, of real movement along a continuum from one position to another. In reality, the entry job is the outcome of a long series of steps. The organization of the series determines which youths obtain which outcomes [p. 266].

> Much has been written about Negro and white youths' entry into the labor force, but surprisingly little is actually known about the process . . . interracial similarities and differences are at present only vaguely understood. Not only is it impossible at this point to indicate, with any clarity and confidence, the causes of racial inequality in the entry process, it is even difficult to describe in any detail the nature and extent of such inequality [p. 264].

OUTLINE OF THIS STUDY

Within the context of previous research efforts and their shortcomings in certain areas, we can now put forward the objectives of this study. This examination of entry into the labor force will describe the first jobs obtained by entrants and the occupational mobility that occurs in the period directly after entry; second, it will evaluate the consequences of the level of entry and the manner in which entry takes place. These mobility processes will be examined in the context of four important individual characteristics: race, family background, educational attainment at entry, and work experiences prior to entry. Multivariate procedures will be employed in every part of the analysis, so as to separate out the influences

of competing causes. The levels of jobs will be measured with a scale of
occupational ranks *and* by their wage rates. Furthermore, educational
attainment will not be fixed at the entry point, and educational mobility
will also be examined.

Description of the Data

This analysis of entry into the labor force is based on a single set of
interviews with a national sample of American men gathered according to
standard multistage procedures by the National Opinion Research Center;
the final selection was made using probability samples. The questionnaire
employed was of a unique design (it is reproduced as Appendix A) and the
reader is urged to examine it before proceeding. This instrument allowed
the interviewer to record continuously a large number of events in the
respondent's life—accurate to the month—over a period stretching from
when he was 14-years old until the time of the interview. For *every* job,
full-time or part-time, held by the respondent, the interviewer recorded
the occupation, industry, wages at the start and at the end of the job,
whether or not it was the individual's own decision to leave the job,
whether or not he had a new job when he left the previous one, the
method used to locate the job, and the extent of on-the-job training. Each
of the respondent's educational experiences was recorded, as were the
composition of the household in which he lived and its geographic location,
his marital status, the jobs held by his wife, and a number of other
variables. In addition, the standard "background" variables were obtained,
including the educational attainment of each parent, the father's occupation, the composition of the household in which the respondent was
raised, and the family's religious affiliation. These interviews constitute a
unique source of information on the experiences of American men. Because of the large number of variables collected and because each one is
defined at every point in time, it is possible to conduct a great variety of
investigations using the data.

The methodological alternative to this procedure of collecting longitudinal data retrospectively is the conventional panel method, in which a
sample of respondents is followed over a period of time, each person being
interviewed several times. The Career Thresholds study uses the latter
technique. Our method has three advantages and two important shortcom-

ings. The greatest difficulty that arises in panel studies is that it is generally impossible to relocate some of the first wave respondents at later points in time. Because it is the most mobile respondents who cannot be found, the traceable individuals constitute a biased sample of the population. Furthermore, there are likely to be some racial and class differences between the respondents who can be followed and those who are lost to the study (see Kohen and Andrisani [1973:17—18] for the rates of attrition in the Career Thresholds study). It is possible to compensate for this difference by making a comparison of the characteristics of the group that can be traced with those of the group that cannot be traced and then weighting the data, but it is not clear whether such a procedure will adequately remove the biases. The retrospective technique cannot lose cases, since only one interview is conducted, and the data are as representative as is permitted by the original sample selection and its nonresponse bias.

The second major advantage of our method is one of cost. The retrospective technique makes possible the collection of longitudinal data covering long periods of time at a far lower cost than a conventional panel study that collects equivalent data—of course, the size of the cost differential varies according to the nature of the instruments used and the number of waves in the panel. Thus, a real comparison of the two methods, holding the *total* cost constant, might allow a researcher using the retrospective technique to interview several times more respondents than his or her counterpart conducting a panel study. Third, the retrospective method makes it possible to gather information on experiences of the respondents that occurred at some time in the past, and to gather it rapidly. Panel studies require the researcher spend a long period of time gathering the data—usually 5 years or more—and do not obtain information previous to the first of the interviews. Often there are important temporal changes in social phenomenon, which make comparisons with earlier conditions of particular interest. Unfortunately, the data available from earlier studies seldom bear closely enough on present research interests to allow good historical comparisons.

The great disadvantage of the retrospective technique lies in the difficulty in estimating how much error is introduced into the data by the faulty memories of respondents. Thus, while the data are far cheaper, they may also be of lower quality. In principle, such data need be no more unreliable than those obtained by the standard items used to measure parental education, or other variables describing earlier points in the respondent's life—although the quality of recall may decline when the respondent is asked to describe many such early events. A quality check on retrospective data is possible by using social security information, school records, personnel files kept by the armed forces, and perhaps other sources. We have not carried out such a check. The one attempt that was made to deal with the problem produced an encouraging result. It was found that, except for black wages, the extent of missing information did not increase significantly when the respondent described events further in his past. Contrary to the procedures used in most interview situations, the respondent was encouraged to have his wife (or parents, if they were in the same household) present during the interview, so that they might provide information that he could not recall. Also, the schedule was designed in such a way that time references could either be to specific ages (as, "I graduated from high school at the age of 19") or to dates ("I joined the army in May 1953"). The second advantage of panel techniques is that they allow the collection of longitudinal data on attitudes, which is not possible using the retrospective method.

Our sample was drawn from the universe of noninstitutionalized men (i.e., not in the armed forces, in prison, or hospitalized), resident in the United States, and between the ages of 30 and 39 in 1968. This age restriction was imposed in order to minimize "cohort effects"—the differences caused by variation in the ages of the respondents and hence in the circumstances of their work experience. The specific range of ages chosen yielded a group of men with enough occupational experience to provide some measures of occupational outcomes as well as information on the entry period itself. The upper age limit was chosen so as to eliminate the direct impact of military service in World War II on the occupational patterns of the men—the oldest respondent was 16-years old in 1945. The interviews were conducted in the spring of 1968.

Blacks were oversampled, in order to facilitate comparisons between blacks and whites. This was accomplished by first selecting a national sample of about 1000 men in which blacks were present according to their proportion in the nation and then adding a separate sample of 600 interviews with black Americans. Of the approximately 1600 respondents, 46% were black. Wherever possible, the race of the respondent was matched to that of the interviewer. Further details about the data collection and processing procedures that were followed are to be found in Blum, Karweit, and Sørenson (1969) and Blum (n.d.).

TABLE 1.1   PROPORTION OF RESPONDENTS IN FIVE CATEGORIES OF EDUCATION,
COMPARED TO PREDICTIONS FROM U.S. CENSUS FOR THE COMPARABLE
AGE COHORT, BY RACE

Race and Education	Distribution (Percent)		Difference (Percent) (1)-(2)	Ratio (1)/(2)
	Sample Survey (1)	U.S. Census† (2)		
White				
No high school	13.6	12.9	.7	1.05
Some high school	14.7	16.7	-2.0**	.88
High school graduate	40.1	43.1	-3.0	.93
Some college	10.9	11.9	-1.0	.92
College graduate	20.7	15.4	5.3*	1.34
Total	100.0	100.0		
Number of cases	850			

$$X^2(4)=20.00*$$

Race and Education				
Black				
No high school	24.0	25.7	-1.7	.93
Some high school	30.9	31.1	-.2	.99
High school graduate	31.0	30.4	.6	1.02
Some college	7.9	7.2	.7	1.10
College graduate	6.2	5.6	.6	1.11
Total	100.0	100.0		
Number of cases	738			

$$X^2(4)=1.85$$

† See U.S. Bureau of the Census (1970b:107)
* Statistically significant at .01
** Statistically significant at .05

In order to make a simple evaluation of the quality of the sample, the observed distribution of educational attainment was compared to that in the national population of American men in the same age range. The result is shown in Table 1.1. For both whites and blacks, there was an oversampling of individuals with high levels of education. The white sample contains 20.7% college graduates, compared to 15.4% in the population; for blacks the sample contains 6.2% college graduates, compared to 5.6% in the population. Chi-square values computed for the two distributions reveal that the white sample is significantly different in educational attainment from the census (at .01); but for blacks the difference is much smaller and not statistically significant. The result is not unexpected—better educated people are easier to locate and interview. These differences will not have much effect on the results of the study, since educational attainment is held constant in almost all of the comparisons.[8] We do have relatively large numbers of missing values for wages, about 10% of the total.

Some Definitions

For the purposes of this analysis, race is defined as a dichotomous variable, with the two categories labelled "black" and "white." Strictly speaking, the latter category consists of non-blacks, for it includes the small numbers of Chicanos, American Indians, and Orientals in the sample; these groups total less than 3% of the "white" group.

It is also necessary to define the meaning of a job, in order to describe occupational mobility. For our purposes, a man changes jobs when he leaves one employer for another or changes occupations, as classified according to the three-digit Census definitions in the U.S. Bureau of the Census (1970), or both. Two measures of the ranking of a given job are used in this analysis, its occupational prestige score and the wages paid to the respondent. The prestige score is based on a ranking of over 300 occupations reported by Siegel (1970:Chap. 2). Blau and Duncan (1967) use socioeconomic rankings of their occupations based on the national distributions of educational attainment and income for those occupations; the measures of education and income all combined, using coefficients derived from a small sample of occupations ranked in a survey (Blau and Duncan 1967:117–128). The prestige scores for all occupations are in Appendix B.

Our prestige scores are "pure" measures of the general view in the population of the social standing of occupations, obtained in a national sample survey. This prestige ranking is known to have remained stable over

[8] There is one exceptional case—in regressions for whites where the college graduates' regression coefficient is very different from those obtained for the lower categories of education. In this case the estimate of the variance explained by education is likely to be too high, because college graduates are over-represented by one third. This effect is only important in the regressions which have occupational prestige scores as the dependent variable. The variance estimates in this case will be of the order of 15% too large.

the past half century and the evaluations show little variation according to the sector of the population ranking the occupations (see Reiss, Duncan, Hatt and North 1961:Chap. 8; Hodge, Siegel, and Rossi 1966). Table 1.2 contains a listing of the prestige scores of some typical occupations. This scale ranks some white collar jobs very close to certain skilled blue collar occupations; service occupations are scattered at different levels, and so on. It is a *continuous* ranking of the prestige accorded occupations by Americans and does not conform to traditional class boundaries. Two more specific points are important. The ranking does include military occupations. The respondents were asked to rate military occupations according to their military rank, rather than to the skill—a corporal who drives a truck is given the prestige score of a corporal, not that of a truck

TABLE 1.2   SOME TYPICAL OCCUPATIONAL PRESTIGE SCORES

Range	Typical Occupations
Above 80.0	Physicians
71.0 - 80.0	Dentists, College Professors, Bankers
60.1 - 70.0	Chemists, Engineers, Teachers
55.1 - 60.0	Accountants, Economists, Postmasters
50.1 - 55.0	Librarians, Technicians
45.1 - 50.0	Musicians, Secretaries, Electricians
40.1 - 45.0	Farm Managers, Farm Owners, Typists, Mailmen, Plumbers
35.1 - 40.0	Clerks, Auto Mechanics
30.1 - 35.0	Cashiers, Bus Drivers, Hairdressers, Farm Foremen
25.1 - 30.0	Retail Salesmen, Operatives, Lowest Ranks of Armed Forces
20.1 - 25.0	Stock Clerks, Housekeepers
15.1 - 20.0	Newsvendors, Peddlers, Wrappers, Bartenders, Farm Laborers
Under 15.1	Bootblacks, Ushers

driver. Second, agricultural occupations are included in the scale; so farm laborers are distinguished from farm owners, with the owners, of course, ranking higher. We are thus able to construct models that include civilian nonfarm occupations *and* farm occupations *and* the ranks of the armed forces. Blau and Duncan's (1967) work excludes the last two groups. Duncan, Featherman, and Duncan (1972:45–49) find that the correlations between pairs of prestige scores and between prestige and other variables are slightly lower than those that would be obtained if the socioeconomic ranking was used instead of prestige. In the small number of cases in which a respondent holds two full-time jobs simultaneously, the one with the greater prestige score is used in the analysis; when the prestige scores are equal, the job with higher wages is chosen.

Unlike the prestige measures, the wage values used are not mean values obtained for the occupation as a whole but are the wages paid to the individual respondent. These wage values were recorded at the start and at the end of each job. All the wage values were standardized to monthly income and were adjusted to yield rates of pay *in constant dollars* (price adjusted, to a 1959 base).[9] This standardization process makes it possible to compare the wage rates of men who entered the labor force during the 15-year period spanned by our respondents. However, the growth in mean *real* wages over the postwar years is a source of unexplained variance in wage values.

Strategy of This Study

We have argued that the first step in any analysis of entry into the labor force must be a clear definition of the meaning of the term *entry*. In Chapter 2 we set out the definition that was applied to our longitudinal records of individual work and educational experiences. The definition makes it possible to define a number of critical variables to describe the entry process: the respondent's education at entry; his age at entry; the first job after entry—and its occupational prestige score, wage rate, and

---

[9] The monthly wage value combines the responses to two items, wage rates (in whatever units they were reported, as hourly, weekly, etc.) and the number of hours worked per week. When the length of the work week was not reported, a mean value was substituted from Department of Labor statistics.

industry; the amount of unemployment before entry; whether the respondent moved between entry and the start of his first job; and so on. The
first analytic task is to examine the relationships among five variables (or
groups of variables) describing the individual as he enters the labor force;
they include his race, family background, age and education at entry, and
the extent of work experience *before* entry. The second part of Chapter 2
relates these variables, and some of the characteristics of the entry process,
to the prestige score and wages of the first job. It then goes on to examine
the relationship between educational attainment and race and the manner
in which entry takes place. Multiple regression techniques are used to
simultaneously evaluate the many different factors affecting job quality.

Chapter 3 covers the 2-year period after entry. Our review of the
research on entry has shown that a critical barrier to the understanding of
the entry process is a lack of knowledge of the mobility processes that
occur just after entry takes place. In tracing our respondents over the
2-year period after entry, we examine the numbers of jobs held, and the
changes in the relative positions of men with different levels of education
and of both races. The regression analysis used to examine the quality of
the first job is repeated, to determine whether there are changes in the
relationship between job quality and individual characteristics during this
time. Some attention is devoted to the respondents who entered the armed
forces and to how their position compares with that of men in the civilian
labor force.

Chapter 4 makes a more detailed examination of job mobility in the
years just after entry. It deals with the consequences of this mobility for
the relative standing of an individual among the group of men with equal
education and of the same race, and touches on differences in the average
mobility of these larger groups. We attempt to discover the factors that
cause an individual to change jobs, differentiating broadly between his
own characteristics—such as his marital status and education—and those of
the situation in which he finds himself—such as the rate of pay of his job.
Second, we measure the results of changing jobs, for it is by no means
certain that the man who switches jobs in the hope of improving his
position does, in fact, succeed in doing so.

Chapter 5, the final chapter of the analysis, deals with the impact of
entry on later occupational and educational achievement. So far, we have
estimates from Blau and Duncan of the impact of the socioeconomic rank
of the first job on later jobs; these longitudinal data allow us to examine

mobility in three dimensions: occupational prestige, wages, and educational attainment in the period after entry. The impact of the first job is also measured in a more comprehensive manner than has so far been possible; in addition to the prestige score and wage level of the first job, a number of other aspects of the entry experience, such as geographical mobility and the effect of entering the armed forces, are examined. A path analysis is presented that summarizes the entry process as a whole. The regressions provide estimates of the net effect of military service on the occupational achievement and educational mobility of the black and white samples as a whole, as well as of the subgroups in five main categories of education.

In almost all cases we present entirely separate analyses of the experiences of white and black entrants, since it cannot be assumed that race does not interact with other variables, such as educational attainment. This separation is required in order to detect racial differences in both the levels of jobs held by blacks and whites and in the stratification *processes.* The inclusion of both races in a single model carries with it the assumption that the impact of race produces only *quantitative* differences in the manner in which individuals move through a *common* entry process. Within each race, it *is* assumed that men with different levels of educational attainment are involved in the same process, though of course men with widely varying amounts of schooling will also differ on a large number of other variables, such as age at entry, parental education, the industry of their jobs, and so on. We did not find any appreciable interaction between educational attainment and the other variables used in the analysis of entry, and this lends support to our decision to separate only the two races. If this study had a vastly larger number of cases, it might be reasonable to construct completely separate models for men at each level of education, within each race.

Limitations of This Study

Before presenting our results, it is useful to set out the limitations of this study, limitations that arise both from the characteristics of the data used and from decisions made in the course of working with this data. The analysis presented here describes men entering the U.S. labor force in the period between the end of World War II and about 1960. It is likely that the patterns observed are at least partially a product of the times: of the changes within the occupational and wage structures during that period, of the migration that took place, of the state of the economy, of the numbers of men who were drafted into or volunteered to serve in the armed forces, and so on. While it may be that some important features of the entry process remain constant over time, it is best to be cautious about making any such claims.

Two of the concerns voiced above, in the section criticizing the research literature, are not spoken to here. The entry process here is considered entirely in individual terms, as a process of personal achievement. Thus, structural changes in the labor force, such as the decrease in the number of farm workers during this period, are conceived in terms of the mobility experienced by the sons of farm workers. Whether these individuals left their fathers' farms out of choice or because they were driven from them by poverty or lack of work is not taken into consideration. Nor do we deal with the perceptions, attitudes, and values of the entrants as they go through these experiences. Yet an understanding of the role played by these factors is necessary if we are to gain a full understanding of the entry process.

A number of limitations arise from the size and nature of the sample. Leaving aside the obvious restriction of these findings to the 30- to 39-year age cohort, the fact that there are only about 800 cases in each of the two racial groups imposes a number of restrictions. For example, only 25 of the black respondents entered the labor force with college degrees. We will show that the differences between whites and blacks vary considerably with educational attainment; so one of the critical comparisons, between white and black college graduates, is on rather shaky statistical legs. A very crude classification of industries is used, simply because there are insufficient cases to support a more detailed analysis. The consideration of geographic migration is limited in just the same way, only about one-tenth of the respondents moved in the period between entry and the start of the first job. As a result, there are too few cases to enable us to do anything more than a crude analysis of the experiences of the migrants, a group that is of considerable sociological interest.

The result of working with this relatively small number of cases is that many small effects appear that border on statistical significance. The temptation is to interpret the findings that "make sense" or that fit in with one's preconceptions, while ignoring those that are not so intellectually manageable. A course of action taken in most government statistical reports, and one that avoids this difficulty, is to ignore all the small differences. In the process, of course, many of the most important and intriguing findings, as well as much of the subtlety of the processes of social stratification under study, disappear. The discussion of the data in this study likely errs on the side of overinterpretation. To protect against this danger we almost always present estimates of the *importance* of an effect (as measured by the variance explained) as well as of the size of the differences observed. In addition, most of the tables include case numbers, so as to remind the reader continuously of the extent of sampling error.

This study does not deal with women; in a sense it contributes to the deplorable tradition among students of social stratification that conceives the mobility process almost entirely in male terms.

Perhaps the most important strategic decision made in the course of the analysis concerns the ranking of occupations. We employ two continuous measures of job equality, prestige scores and wages, exclusively. so there is no discussion of the transitions among farm, blue-collar, and white-collar jobs, or within some more complex discrete classification. These two sorts of analysis are complementary. We have chosen to use the continuous measures for two reasons: The occupational mobility processes that occur in the period after entry are relatively small in magnitude, and the use of continuous variables allows us to measure them accurately. The total number of respondents is simply not large enough to provide the basis for an analysis of transitions within a set of class categories. Second, the use of these continuous measures makes it possible to employ multivariate methods, particularly regression and path analysis, which cannot be used easily when the dependent variable is measured as a set of loosely ordered categories.

Finally, we should acknowledge that the concerns which motivate this study are primarily sociological and that sociological bias is present: in the literature that has been examined, in the formulation of research objectives, in the choice of analytic methods and of the variables used, and in the conclusions reached. We have attempted to speak to the concerns of labor economists, the group that has probably devoted the most energy to dealing with entry into the labor force, but researchers from that discipline would, no doubt, have treated these data in a different way.

Entering the Labor Force 2

This chapter begins with a definition of entry into the labor force that, when applied to our longitudinal records of educational and work experiences, makes it possible to create the variables describing the entry process. The first part of the analysis concerns the relationships among race, family background, education at entry, age at entry, and work experiences *before* an individual enters the labor force. After an examination of the roles played by race and by the characteristics of the family in which the respondent grew up in determining the amount of education with which he starts work, these variables and age at entry are combined in an analysis of the number of full-time and part-time jobs held before entry, and of the prestige scores and wages of those jobs. A path analysis is presented to show the process as a whole.

The level of the first job is commonly considered to be the most important single measure describing the way in which entry occurs. After taking a detailed look at the prestige score and starting wages of this first job and their relation to the respondent's educational attainment, we describe a number of other aspects of the way in which entry takes place. These include the extent of unemployment between the point at which an individual leaves school and the start of his first job, his marital status at the time, geographic mobility in the interval before entry, the way in which the first job is located, whether or not the first job is in the armed forces, and the industry of the first job. The objective of this description is to determine the extent to which blacks and whites, men at each level of education, begin their careers in different ways, as well as at the different levels, as measured by prestige scores and wages. Finally, the variables describing the mode of entry are combined with three other predictors of entry level: family background, education, and the amount of work experience before entry, in a multiple regression analysis of the level of entry.

So, we bring the analysis of entry up to the point at which the respondents have started their first jobs. The next chapter goes on to deal with the course of the first job and the 2-year period after entry.

DEFINITION OF ENTRY

There is necessarily a certain degree of arbitrariness in any definition of entry into the labor force. While in the majority of cases the point at which an individual makes a firm commitment to the work force is unmistakable—he leaves fulltime schooling and does not return—for some careers the issue is more problematic. Men who return to the status of full-time student or who get their first jobs in the armed forces pose the difficulty. What constitutes this commitment to the labor force? It is easier to approach the problem by describing what we do not mean by entry. A full-time summer job cannot signify entry. Nor can the definition be tied to age, since men enter the labor force at very different times, according to their levels of education and when they started school. We made the somewhat arbitrary decision that a person who leaves school for one year and then returns has *not* entered the labor force. The definition finally arrived at is as follows: *A man is said to have entered the labor force when he leaves full-time schooling and participates in the labor force for a period of more than 16 months without returning to full-time education during that time.* The reason for the choice of a 16-month interval is that it is the maximum time covered by one school year plus the preceding and following summers. To participate, the respondent had to be holding a full-time job or be engaged in looking for a full-time job; men who were not looking for work, who took part-time jobs without seeking full-time work, or who stayed out of the labor force because of illness or for some other reason had not entered. Since the labor force status variable is recorded on the questionnaire, there was no need to make any assumptions about when an individual was actually looking for work.

The definition is not restricted to the civilian labor force; a respondent who joined the armed forces also entered the labor force, since the minimum period of army service was 2 years. We differ from Blau and Duncan (1967:446) in this respect, since they asked the respondent to exclude military service when identifying the first job. Our ground for doing so was simply the fact that military service represents a decisive break with the experience of being a full-time student. It does not seem reasonable to compare the first civilian job of an individual who has spent 3 years in the armed forces, away from school and his family of origin, with the first job of a person who has just left high school. Men whose first jobs are in the armed forces likely undergo many of the same kinds of personal changes as those whose first jobs are in civilian life. For example, the decision to return to school, although it may be facilitated by the financial aid available to veterans, marks no less a break from the life of the average soldier than it does from civilian work experiences.

The definition of entry admits of no proof; there are certainly other reasonable definitions. For Blau and Duncan's purpose, that of creating models of the whole of the occupational stratification process, their definition may make more sense—at least a good argument could be made in support of it. An analysis of our data using Blau and Duncan's definition of entry can be found in Coleman, Blum, Sørensen, and Rossi (1972), in Blum (1972), and in Coleman, Berry, and Blum (1972). However, for our investigation of the entry process itself, the one proposed here seems more reasonable. And this is the only claim we can make on its behalf, that it is a sensible way to proceed.

CHARACTERISTICS OF INDIVIDUALS AT ENTRY

Education Attainment and Age

In terms of its impact on later occupational achievement, the single most important characteristic of a man who enters the labor force is his level of educational attainment. Certainly it has drawn great attention from researchers. Distributions of education in the white and black samples are shown in Table 2.1. One-quarter of the black respondents begin their careers without ever having attended high school, compared to 15.5% of the whites; just over one-half of the whites, but only one-third of blacks, graduate from high school; 10.7% of the whites complete college,

TABLE 2.1   EDUCATION AT ENTRY, BY RACE

Education at Entry	Percentage Distribution		Score on 0 to 10 Scale	Five Category Classifi-cation
	White	Black		
Less than 5 years	1.6	4.7	0	First
5-7 years	4.7	13.1	1	First
Elementary school graduate	9.2	7.1	2	First
Total with no high school	15.5	24.9		
Some high school	21.0	35.2	3	Second
High school graduate	42.2	29.4	4	Third
High school graduate and some vocational	.7	.6	5	Third
Total high school graduate	42.9	30.0		
Some college	9.8	6.5	6	Fourth
College graduate	7.9	8.3	7	Fifth
Master's degree	1.2	.1	8	Fifth
Some graduate or professional	.1	.0	9	Fifth
Graduate or professional degree	1.5	.0	10	Fifth
Total college graduate	10.7	3.4		
Total	100.0	100.0		
Number of cases	850	738		

compared to just 3.4% of the blacks. Another way of making this compari-son is by examining the "completion rates" for individuals who begin to attend high school and college before entering the labor force. Of the whites who start high school, three-quarters graduate before beginning to work while only one-half of the blacks do so. Of the whites who start college, one-half graduate before entry; only one-third of the blacks are able to graduate. The gap between the two races is by no means exagger-ated by some peculiarity of the definition of entry into the labor force. As we shall see, it *widens* in the years after entry, since whites are also more likely than blacks to get additional educational experience after entry.

As could be expected from the difference in education at entry, the average black respondent enters the labor force about 1 year earlier than his white counterpart; the mean ages at entry are 17.3 and 18.3 years, respectively. Seventeen percent of the blacks are at least 20 years of age at entry, compared to 26% of the whites; conversely, 26% of the blacks enter

TABLE 2.2 MEAN, MEDIAN, AND STANDARD DEVIATION OF AGE AT ENTRY, BY EDUCATION AT ENTRY AND RACE

Education at Entry	Mean (years)		Median (years)		Standard Deviation (years)		Number of cases	
	White	Black	White	Black	White	Black	White	Black
No high school	15.6	15.0	15.3	15.0	1.64	1.87	132	184
Some high school	16.7	17.1	16.9	17.0	1.18	1.81	179	260
High school graduate	18.1	18.4	18.1	18.3	0.90	1.33	365	221
Some college	19.9	20.1	19.8	19.9	1.45	1.81	83	48
College graduate	23.3	22.1	22.9	21.9	1.80	1.14	91	25
Total	18.0	17.3	18.0	17.3	2.64	2.40	850	738

before the age of 16, compared to 17% of the whites. The racial difference in the age at entry disappears when education at entry is held constant. As Table 2.2 reveals, within each level of educational attainment, the mean ages at entry are almost identical for whites and blacks. The only differences are found in the lowest and highest categories, where the composition of the groups is not the same for both races. Thus, in the "college graduate" category, one-quarter of the whites have advanced degrees, but almost all of the blacks have only first degrees—hence the average age at entry is greater for whites because of their higher level of schooling. The very small differences between the mean and median ages at entry, at all levels of education and for both races, show that the age distributions are very symmetric.

The relationship between education and age at entry is very strong; the simple correlations are 0.893 for whites and 0.698 for blacks. The difference in these correlations is no artifact of the difference in the distributions of education at entry, for within four of the levels of education the variation in age is greater for blacks (although not in the highest group, where the distributions of attainment are different). The implication would seem to be that whites' school experiences are more regular, that they are less disrupted by failure in a grade or by the experience of being placed in a grade with mostly older students. Parnes *et al.* (1970:21) reach the same conclusion when they examine the ages of black and white youths still in school. They observe a greater age dispersion among black youths within the five categories of education used here; they also find that blacks at a given level of schooling are older than their white counterparts, but the difference is very small, amounting to no more than .3 years.

In order to determine the relationship between educational attainment at entry and class background, four measures describing the family in which the respondent was raised were inserted into a multiple regression.[1] They include the educational attainment of the respondent's father and of his mother, the prestige score of the father's occupation when the respondent was 14 years of age, and the number of children in the family.

---

[1] There are some missing values for each of the variables. In order to overcome this difficulty, the regressions were computed from a "pairwise present" correlation matrix. In such a matrix each correlation coefficient is based on the subset of respondents for which neither of the required pair of variables has a missing value.

TABLE 2.3 REGRESSION OF EDUCATION AT ENTRY ON FAMILY BACKGROUND, BY RACE

Independent Variable	Regression Coefficient		Standardized Regression Coefficient		Simple Correlation with Respondent's Education		Mean Value	
	White	Black	White	Black	White	Black	White	Black
Father's education	.184	.075	.204*	.077	.422	.328	2.40	1.66
Mother's education	.161	.264	.151*	.244*	.395	.363	2.79	2.16
Father's occupation	.0228	.0142	.156*	.107*	.366	.246	36.1	28.2
Number of siblings	-.123	-.056	-.200*	-.141*	-.332	-.227	3.64	5.35
Regression constant	2.71*	2.39*						
Percent of variance explained by all variables	27.0*	17.2*						

* Statistically significant at .01

Educational attainment is measured on the 10-point scale described in Table 2.1. The results of the regressions, performed separately for whites and blacks, are shown in Table 2.3. The four family background variables explain 27.0% of the variation in the respondent's educational attainment for whites, but significantly less, 17.2%, for blacks. Thus blacks could not be as certain of "converting" the "assets" of their families, such as the high levels of education of their parents, into increased education for themselves.

Three of the measures of family background, the education of each parent and the father's occupational prestige score, are positively related to the respondent's education; the fourth, the number of siblings, has a *negative* effect, so that individuals with a larger number of brothers and sisters enter with comparatively less education. There are important racial differences in the relative effects of the four family background variables. For whites, each unit of father's education adds .184 units of schooling to that of his son, holding the other three variables constant, whereas the corresponding figure for blacks is only .075. This pattern is reversed for the mother's education, where each unit adds .161 units to the son's education for whites and .264 for blacks. Also, the detrimental effect of larger families is more strongly felt by whites, and the father's occupation has a greater impact on whites' education. These findings suggest that there are structural differences between white and black families that effect the way in which parental characteristics are transmitted from one generation to the next.

It is useful to compare these results with those obtained by Duncan (1967), although in her analysis a variable describing whether the individual was raised in an "intact family" takes the place of mother's education. Though there are a number of differences between her sample and this one, and in the variables used, a direct comparison appears justified.[2] For

---

[2] Duncan (1967) uses the data from the Occupational Changes in the Generation study reported more fully in Blau and Duncan (1967). The results most comparable to those presented here are for whites aged 16 between 1946 and 1950 and for non-whites aged 16 between 1941 and 1950; her sample includes only the native-born. The differences between variables include: Duncan uses a socioeconomic ranking of occupations, we use prestige scores; her values of education are measured in years of attainment, not on the 10-point scale used here; her respondent's education is a final attainment, our measure is attainment at entry, and may increase during a respondent's career. It is encouraging to note that Duncan's values for the number of

the cohort most comparable in age to this one, the father's education and occupation, the number of siblings, and "intact family" explain 27.9% of the variation in whites' education, 13.6% in that of non-whites. The small differences between these values and the corresponding values 27.0% and 17.2% obtained here, fall almost to zero when the one noncomparable variable is removed from each of the regressions. For whites, the relative effects of the variables in the two studies are quite similar, but our inclusion of mother's education gives us a lower estimate of the effect of father's occupation.[3]

There are substantial differences between the two studies' results for blacks (Duncan's "non-whites"). Since we find that mother's education has the largest single effect on the black respondent's education, in models that do not include this variable, its effect is partly measured by other variables, primarily father's occupation and education. Duncan does obtain larger standardized regression coefficients for these two variables, .26 and .22; our corresponding values are .108 and .078. Thus, the addition of the mother's education to the conventional models, which include only the father's characteristics, seems very productive, particularly for non-white populations.

The difference in the mean education attainment of the races can be analyzed in terms of two major factors: The fact that blacks come from homes that are generally poorer than those of whites, and racial differences in the social process of converting parental advantages into increased education. Using the mean values of the family background variables and the regression coefficients, it is possible to measure these two effects. The mean education at entry, measured on the 10-point scale, is 3.16 for blacks and 3.89 for whites, a difference of .73 units. Both values fall between "some high school" (scored 3) and "high school graduate" (scored 4). Now, the substitution of the higher average values of the four background variables from the white sample into the black regression

---

siblings are similar to ours. Duncan finds that the average number of siblings is 3.8 for whites and 5.5 for nonwhites. We obtain values of 3.64 and 5.35 for non-blacks and blacks respectively.

[3] Duncan's standardized regression coefficients (1967:366) are, for whites, .22 for father's education, .08 for intact family, −.22 for number of siblings, and .26 for father's occupation; for nonwhites the corresponding values are .24, .10, −.04, and .16.

equation, raises the mean value of black attainment by .42, to 3.58. Alternatively, if the conversion *processes* are equilibrated, by substituting the black means into the white regression equation, the mean black attainment increases by .19, to 3.35 units of education. Now the sum of the two increments is .61 units, or .12 units less than the observed difference of .73 units. This remaining portion must be attributed to the interaction of the background deficits and processual differences. Thus, the largest part of the difference in the educational attainment of whites and blacks is due to the poorer family backgrounds of the latter and not to racial differences in the ability to convert these attributes into education.

If we are prepared to accept the regression model for whites as predominating in the society, then the contributions of each of the four variables to the racial difference can be easily calculated.[4] Of the .73 units of difference, .14 is due to father's education, .10 to mother's education, .18 to father's occupation, and .21 to number of siblings; the remaining .10 is the "pure" effect of discrimination, which cannot be allocated to any of the four variables. Using only two variables, Duncan (1968:98) finds that about one-half of the educational difference can be attributed to the father's occupation and number of siblings; our four-variable model attributes three-quarters of the racial difference to background variables. This unaccounted for remainder must not be taken as the only effect of racial discrimination, for the differences in family background that are responsible for the larger part of the racial difference are just as surely the result of racism.

Jobs Held before Entry into the Labor Force

Many of our respondents have some work experience when they enter the labor force, mostly full-time summer jobs and part-time jobs during the school year. The duration, numbers, occupations and wages of

[4] The difference due to father's education, for example, is obtained by multiplying the difference between the mean values of this variable for blacks and whites by the white regression coefficient for father's education. In this case, it is (2.41– 1.66) times .184, or .14. This procedure assumes that all four of the family background variables converge simultaneously on the respondents and that there is no causal structure among them.

these jobs were recorded on the questionnaire, so it is possible to examine both the extent of this job experience before entry and the kinds of jobs that were held. Since the holding of full-time and part-time jobs may not have the same meaning, the two categories are treated separately in this discussion. While the great majority of the full-time jobs preceding entry into the labor force were held during summer, a few men held such jobs while simultaneously attending school, and a few more held full-time jobs during a 1-year interruption of their full-time study (since a person in the last category had not, by our definition, entered the labor force).

Three important questions arise with regard to these early occupational experiences. The simplest is descriptive. What proportion of individuals hold jobs before entry and what kinds of jobs are held before entry? Second, how do the number and the quality of these jobs relate to the characteristics of the individuals who hold them? It is reasonable to predict that men who enter the labor force when they are older and who have more education at entry should have had a larger number of pre-entry jobs. Without analyzing the data, however, it is not possible to predict how strongly number of jobs will be related to age and education at entry. Finally, what is the impact of family background on the number of pre-entry jobs held? Since men from more privileged backgrounds obtain more education and enter later, it can be argued that they should have a larger number of jobs. But with education and age at entry held constant, perhaps poorer respondents, whose families have the greatest need, will be more likely to work. The analysis will resolve this question. Of more interest in terms of understanding the stratification process as a whole is the question of whether these early work experiences do anything to affect the quality of *later* jobs. This last problem will be dealt with in the multivariate analysis of the quality of first job and in subsequent chapters focusing on later occupational achievement.

Just over one-third of the whites and one-seventh of the blacks hold one or more full-time jobs before they enter the labor force. Table 2.4 shows that the probability of holding such a job is very strongly influenced by the age at which a man enters the labor force and by his education at that point—which is only natural, since older and better educated individuals have better opportunities to find summer jobs. However, holding age or education at entry constant, whites are approximately twice as likely as blacks to have held one or more full-time jobs. Fully 90% of white college graduates and 38% of white high school graduates have at least one

TABLE 2.4   NUMBER OF FULL-TIME JOBS BEFORE ENTRY, BY EDUCATION AT
            ENTRY AND RACE

	Part-time Jobs before Entry			
	Percent Holding One or More Jobs		Mean Number of Jobs Held	
Education or Age at Entry	White	Black	White	Black
Education at entry				
No high school	8	4	.13	.07
Some high school	21	11	.46	.23
High school graduate	38	19	1.08	.58
Some college	66	36	2.39	1.08
College graduate	90	44	4.68	1.68
Total	38	14	1.31	.40
Percent of variance explained by education			36.7*	8.7*
Age at entry				
No high school	9	3	.13	.03
Some high school	16	7	.34	.12
High school graduate	30	15	.71	.32
Some college	40	14	1.21	.33
College graduate	74	34	3.19	1.24
Total	38	14	1.31	.40
Percent of variance explained by age			29.3*	12.0*

* Statistically significant at .001

such job, while the corresponding proportions for blacks are 44% and 19%.
An examination of the average number of jobs held before entry reveals
the same pattern, though the racial difference is somewhat larger. Whites
hold an average of 1.31 jobs each before entry—ranging from a mean of
0.13 jobs for those who enter with no high school, to 1.08 jobs for high
school graduates, to 4.68 jobs for college graduates. The average black
respondent holds .40 jobs before entry, and the mean number of jobs for
men with no high school is .07, for high school graduates .58; and for
college graduates 1.68.

An analysis of variance reveals that education at entry, broken into five categories, explains 46.7% of the variation in the number of full-time jobs held before entry by whites, but only 8.7% for blacks. The five categories of age at entry explain 29.3% of the variation for whites, 12.0% for blacks. The far lower proportion of explained variance for blacks derives partly from racial differences in the distributions of age and education at entry, while the highly skewed distribution of the dependent variable—a majority of the respondents hold no such job and those who do usually hold only one or two jobs—drives down the variance for both races.

The relationships between the number of full-time jobs held and education and age at entry are best measured by the correlations among them, rather than by an analysis of variance with a small number of categories, which restricts the range of the independent variable. Using the correlation coefficients, age at entry explains 37.0% of the variation in the number of full-time jobs for whites, and education accounts for 33.8%. For blacks, the values are 11.1% and 7.4%. So, the extent of job holding is somewhat more tightly tied to age at entry, which is a measure of exposure to the labor market, rather than to education. Of course, age at entry is very strongly related to education at entry, and the two variables are difficult to distinguish in practice. In order to examine more closely the influence of these two variables, and to introduce the effect of the four measures of family background, the number of jobs was regressed on these variables simultaneously. In order to use both the age and education variables, with their very high intercorrelations, dummy variables were used to separate the men with the least education, no high school, from four groups, and to distinguish men who enter the labor force before the age of 16 from the groups entering at the ages of 16, 17, 18, and 19 or more. The regression is shown in Table 2.5.

The effect of family background on job holding is very weak when education and age at entry are held constant; the four variables raise the explained variance in the number of jobs held by 0.5% for whites, by 0.6% for blacks. Only two of the regression coefficients are statistically significant; whites with fewer siblings hold more jobs, as do blacks with *lower* father's education. These results weakly support the theory that whites having more jobs tend to come from higher status homes, while blacks in poorer situations work because of need. But the main finding is that family background has almost no independent effect on the number of jobs held.

TABLE 2.5   REGRESSION OF THE NUMBER OF FULL-TIME JOBS BEFORE ENTRY ON FAMILY
BACKGROUND, EDUCATION AT ENTRY, AND AGE AT ENTRY, BY RACE

Independent Variable	Regression Coefficient		Standardized Regression Coefficient		Unique Variance Explained (Percent)	
	White	Black	White	Black	White	Black
Family background					.5	.6
Father's education	-.01	-.08	-.009	-.101		
Mother's education	.04	.04	.034	.043		
Father's occupation	.00	.00	.009	.027		
Number of siblings	-.05	.01	-.062	.019		
Education at entry					8.0	1.0
Some high school	-.03	.05	-.005	.020		
High school graduate	.18	.23	.040	.082		
Some college	.91	.44	.122	.085		
College graduate	3.02	.82	.419	.118		
Age at entry					2.1	3.9
Sixteen	.12	.05	.018	.015		
Seventeen	.31	.20	.060	.067		
Eighteen	.71	.18	.132	.052		
Nineteen or more	1.40	.89	.278	.285		
Regression constant	.03	-.01				
Percent variance explained by all variables	39.2	13.4				

*   Statistically significant at .05

Rather larger proportions of men hold part-time jobs before entry
than hold full-time jobs. Just less than one-half of the whites and one-
quarter of the blacks hold at least one such job (compared to the 38.1% of
whites and 14.1% of blacks that hold full-time jobs). The correlation
coefficients show that educational attainment at entry explains 15.4% of
the variance in the number of part-time jobs for whites and 5.4% for
blacks; age at entry explains 15.9% for whites and 5.8% for blacks. So, the
number of part-time jobs before entry is less closely tied to age and
education at entry than is full-time job holding. In part, the lower
explained variances are due to the fact that a single part-time job can be
held for a very long time, while almost all the full-time jobs before entry
last between 2 and 4 months, since they are summer jobs. Again, age and

education have about equal predictive power. The results are shown in Table 2.6.

Let us now examine the prestige scores and wages of these jobs held before entry, again treating the full-time jobs first. Individuals who held no jobs, 61.8% of the whites and 85.9% of the blacks, are entirely excluded from the analysis, drastically cutting down the number of cases available. A further difficulty is presented by the fact that among the men who had some full-time work experience before entry, some held several jobs while others held only one or two jobs. In order to create a single measure of the prestige score of the varying number of jobs held by different respondents,

TABLE 2.6   NUMBER OF PART-TIME JOBS BEFORE ENTRY, BY EDUCATION AT ENTRY AND RACE

| | Part-time Jobs before Entry | | | |
| | Percent Holding One or More Jobs | | Mean Number of Jobs Held | |
Education or Age at Entry	White	Black	White	Black
Education at entry				
No high school	18	9	.21	.11
Some high school	38	25	.65	.36
High school graduate	52	34	1.22	.76
Some college	66	27	1.48	.75
College graduate	66	60	1.73	1.12
Total	47	25	1.13	.47
Percent of variance explained by education			14.1*	6.3*
Age at entry				
No high school	19	12	.23	.15
Some high school	39	16	.65	.24
High school graduate	47	24	.98	.39
Some college	55	31	1.41	.59
College graduate	59	43	1.88	1.05
Total	47	29	1.13	.47
Percent of variance explained by age			10.0*	8.1*

* Statistically significant at .001

TABLE 2.7   WEIGHTED MEANS OF OCCUPATIONAL PRESTIGE AND WAGES OF FULL-TIME
            JOBS BEFORE ENTRY, BY EDUCATION AT ENTRY AND RACE

Education at Entry	Weighted Mean of Occupational Prestige		Weighted Mean of Wages ($/month)		Number of cases†	
	White	Black	White	Black	White	Black
No high school	20.7	18.9	125	130	10	7
Some high school	23.1	21.4	189	170	33	26
High school graduate	22.9	21.1	190	164	125	37
Some college	26.2	24.6	217	209	53	16
College graduate	30.9	23.9	236	230	80	11
Total	25.4	21.9	205	179	323	104
Percent of variance explained by education	13.9*	5.1	4.4*	6.7		

* Statistically significant at .05
† Because of missing values, the number of wage values is about ten percent
  less than the number of prestige values; there are 299 wage values for
  whites, 95 for blacks.

the prestige scores of all the jobs held by an entrant were averaged, with
each prestige score weighted according to the duration of the job.[5] This
procedure will tend to cut down the magnitude of the observed differences
in prestige scores among men at different levels of education. For example,
if a college graduate held a high prestige job in the summer before
graduation, its impact is likely to be diminished by earlier jobs with lower
prestige scores.

   These pre-entry full-time jobs were quite poor ones. The tabulation
of the prestige averages in Table 2.7 reveals that, for whites, the lowest
value for those who entered with no high school was only 20.7 prestige
points, approximately that of an unskilled laborer. The average score for all

   [5] To take a concrete example, if a man held three jobs, with durations of 2, 4,
and 3 months, and they had prestige scores of 30, 25 and 35 respectively, then the
weighted prestige average would be equal to (2 months × 30 points + 4 months × 25
points + 3 months × 35 points) all divided by (2 + 4 + 3) months, or 29.4 points.

the jobs held by men who graduated from college was 30.9, about that of a factory operative. For blacks, the means are lower and the range is much more restricted, from 18.9 to 23.9 prestige points. Thus, not only do blacks hold far fewer jobs before entry, even with age and educational attainment at entry held constant, but the jobs they hold are of significantly lower quality. The racial gap between the mean prestige values grows with increasing education.

This prestige average was regressed on groups of dummy variables describing the respondent's educational attainment and age at entry, the four measures of family background, and the number of full-time jobs held before entry (in Table 2.8). Together, all the variables explain 17.9% of the variance in the prestige average for whites, 18.9% for blacks. The small numbers of cases used in this regression, particularly for blacks, make the results very prone to error. However, some interesting patterns appear. Though the total explained variances are very similar for blacks and whites, the relative strengths of the four factors differ considerably according to race. The family background variables have little influence on whites' prestige averages, but for blacks the four variables uniquely explain 6.1% of the variation in prestige—with the mother's education having the strongest effect. The effect of education at entry is much stronger for whites, where it uniquely explains 7.1% of the variance in the prestige average, compared to only 1.7% for blacks. Age at entry, the best measure of exposure of the labor market in the period before entry, explains 5.0% of the variance in prestige for blacks but an insignificant 0.3% for whites. So, blacks who were older when they entered found better jobs, while whites with better credentials, as measured by more education, obtained better jobs. The number of jobs held in this period is *negatively* related to their average quality, for both races. Comparing individuals with equal education at entry, it appears that a man with fewer jobs, which he likely held just in the 2 or 3 years before entry, is likely to have held higher prestige jobs, since he avoided the poorer jobs he might have obtained when he was younger and less educated.

The weighted wage averages (using the mean of the wage values at the start and at the end of each job) of the full-time jobs held before entry are also very low, ranging from about $125 per month (1959 dollars) for men who enter with no high school, to $175 per month for high school graduates, to $235 per month for college graduates. Race has little impact on these values (the averages are in Table 2.7). Regressing the wage

TABLE 2.8 REGRESSION OF OCCUPATIONAL PRESTIGE OF FULL-TIME JOBS BEFORE ENTRY ON FAMILY BACKGROUND, EDUCATION AT ENTRY, AGE AT ENTRY, AND THE NUMBER OF FULL-TIME JOBS BEFORE ENTRY, BY RACE, FOR MEN WITH ONE OR MORE FULL-TIME JOBS BEFORE ENTRY

Independent Variable	Regression Coefficient		Standardized Regression Coefficient		Unique Variance Explained (percent)	
	Whites	Blacks	Whites	Blacks	Whites	Blacks
Family background						
Father's education	.22	.22	.05	.05	1.0	6.1
Mother's education	.13	.87	.02	.20		
Father's occupation	.02	.05	.02	.09		
Number of siblings	-.24	.20	-.06	.10		
Education at entry						
Some high school	1.8	.6	.06	.04	7.1	1.7
High school graduate	.8	-.7	.04	-.05		
Some college	4.4	2.5	.18	.14		
College graduate	10.0	2.3	.47	.10		
Age at entry						
Sixteen	-.7	-1.4	-.02	-.05	0.3	5.0
Seventeen	1.4	-2.0	.06	-.12		
Eighteen	2.1	3.0	.09	-.17		
Nineteen or more	1.6	.5	.09	.04		
Number of full-time jobs	-.8	-4.7				
Regression constant	21.8	17.5				
Percent of variance explained by all variables	17.9	18.9				
Number of cases	324	104				

* Statistically significant at .05

averages on the four factors used in the prestige analysis above explains 8.9% of variance in wages for whites and 30.0% for blacks. Again, the unique effect of the variables describing family background is far greater for blacks; they explain 13.6% of the variance, versus 0.6% for whites. In contrast to the prestige results, the impact of age at entry on the wage average is far larger than that of education at entry for *both* whites and blacks. Thus the education of the respondent apparently has far less to do with the wages he receives than does his age. Older boys are better paid.

Prestige and wage averages for the part-time jobs held before entry were calculated in the same fashion as for the full-time jobs. The results are less interesting. The prestige averages increase with educational attainment at entry, although the major difference in the quality of these jobs is between the college graduates and all four of the lower categories of education (see Table 2.9). The wage means are very low, and blacks are paid *more* than whites, $100.2 versus $85.4 per month! These wage averages do not vary significantly with the respondent's education at entry, they explain only 1.7% in the variance for whites and 2.7% for

TABLE 2.9   WEIGHTED MEANS OF OCCUPATIONAL PRESTIGE AND WAGES OF PART-TIME JOBS BEFORE ENTRY, BY EDUCATION AT ENTRY AND RACE

Education at Entry	Weighted Mean of Occupational Prestige		Weighted Mean of Wages ($/month)		Number of cases†	
	White	Black	White	Black	White	Black
No high school	21.4	18.9	118.5	99.5	23	16
Some high school	20.0	20.9	83.8	106.7	67	63
High school graduate	23.0	19.9	79.8	89.9	186	75
Some college	23.4	18.8	79.3	94.8	55	13
College graduate	29.1	27.1	97.5	129.7	60	15
Total	23.4	20.7	85.4	100.2	391	182
Percent of variance explained by education	10.0*	8.5	1.7	2.7		

* Statistically significant at .05
† Because of missing values, the number of wage values is about ten percent less than the number of prestige values; there are 345 wage values for whites, 156 for blacks.

blacks. Indeed, the highest-paid white group is the one with the *least* education! This suggests that some characteristic of the job, rather than of the respondent, is responsible for determining the rate of pay. Should it be that the best indicator of the rate of pay is simply the number of hours worked, our method would be unable to explain differences in this variable. This seems a reasonable explanation for the unusual results.

A number of generalizations emerge from this analysis of the jobs held before entry into the labor force. Whites are much more likely to have worked before entry; even with age and education held constant they hold twice as many such jobs as blacks. The number of jobs is more predictable for whites than for blacks. These pre-entry jobs generally require few skills and have low rates of pay. There is a tendency for age at entry and family background to play a more important role in determining the quality of the jobs held by blacks, for education to have a stronger effect in the case of whites. This suggests that whites can trade on their educational qualifications to get better jobs, but that blacks have better jobs if they are in the labor market for a longer period. This, in turn, implies that the whites who hold jobs may do so for different reasons than blacks, and that economic necessity may provide more of a motivation for black job-holders. Finally, it appears that the dynamics of part-time job holding are not the same as those of full-time job holding, particularly as regards the quality of the jobs.

Path Analysis Up to the Entry Point

In order to integrate these findings about the relationships among the variables defined up to the point when the individual enters the labor force, they have been placed in a path analysis, again separately for whites and blacks (see Figure 2.1). One group of variables, measuring the prestige scores and wages of the pre-entry jobs, has been omitted, because their values are not defined for the large part of the sample who held no job before entry. Since the causal ordering of the variables is not problematic—because of their temporal arrangement—the purpose of presenting the path diagrams is illustrative rather than analytical. Paths without statistically significant effects, at .05, were deleted.

The temporal order of the number of pre-entry jobs and educational attainment is not immediately obvious. The jobs are held before entry, and

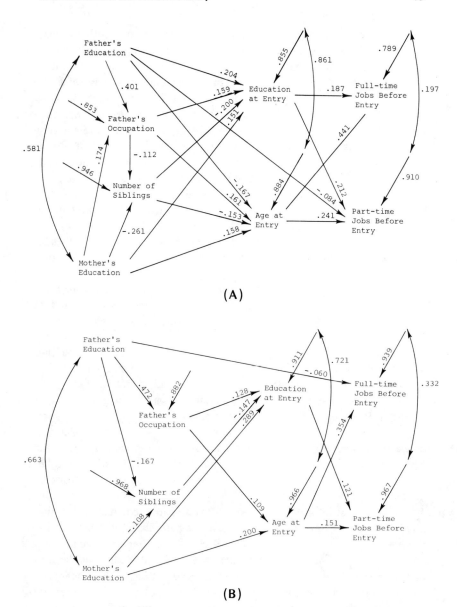

Figure 2.1. Path model to the point of entry (a) whites and (b) blacks.

hence before the educational attainment at entry is defined; both variables change simultaneously in the pre-entry period. It is easier to ask which one *causes* the other. Do more jobs lead to increased education or does more education result in more jobs? The first alternative holds true only if pre-entry job holding contributes to prolonging the time in school. This may be the case for some respondents, particularly college students who are unable to continue their education without such earnings. However, our data suggest that this is not a common pattern; over one-half of the respondents hold only one or two such jobs, and it does not seem reasonable to assume that they decisively influence the amount of schooling obtained. It is clearly true that increased education does lead to increased pre-entry job holding—both because individuals acquire greater skills and because they remain eligible for these jobs for a longer time. So we assume that education occurs first, while acknowledging that this ordering, though a good one, is an imperfect approximation of the true circumstances.

The path diagrams show a number of important features of the entry process. The structure of the family background effects is different for each race. For the whites, there is no direct effect of father's education on the number of siblings; for blacks, there are no paths from mother's education to father's occupation, or from father's occupation to the number of siblings. In the diagram for whites, all four of the family background variables directly influence both age and education at entry; in the diagram for blacks, only mother's education and father's occupation directly affect age at entry, and father's education exerts only an indirect influence on education at entry. In both cases, the very high correlations between age and education at entry are only in small part due to their common relationship to family background—the correlations between the residuals for education and age at entry are .861 for whites and .721 for blacks.

The greater impact of age at entry, as compared to education, on the number of jobs before entry is clear from the path diagrams, although the difference is more pronounced for blacks. In both cases the father's education has a negative effect on one of the pre-entry job variables, on part-time jobs for whites, and on full-time jobs for blacks. This supports the argument that economic necessity, and not ambition, drives men to work when education and age are held constant. However, the impact of father's education is very small. The other family background variables exert only indirect effects on pre-entry jobs, through age and education at entry. The correlations between the number of full-time and part-time jobs before entry cannot be fully explained by their common relationships to earlier variables; the correlations between their residuals are calculated as .197 for whites and .332 for blacks.

THE FIRST JOB AFTER ENTRY

Discussion of the first job after entry proceeds in three stages. The first section describes the occupational prestige scores and starting wages of the first job[6] and closely examines their relationship to educational attainment at entry and race. The next section describes a number of less-hierarchical aspects of entry, the extent of unemployment before entry, marital status at entry, geographic moves before the first job is found, and their distances, how the job was located, whether the first job was in the armed forces, and the industry in which it is situated. The concluding section takes these features of the first job, together with three groups of variables described in the first section—family background, the number of jobs held before entry, and education at entry—and combines them in a regression analysis of the prestige score and wages of the first job.

Prestige Scores and Starting Wages

The mean occupational prestige score of the first job is 29.3 for whites, compared to 24.8 for blacks—this difference, in terms of the way occupations generally are perceived, is quite small. Among men with no high school there is only a small difference (averaging about one prestige point) between the two races. At higher levels of education the gap between whites and blacks widens considerably. Thus, as shown in Table 2.10, the mean prestige score of white high-school graduates is 28.2, compared to 26.0 for blacks, and the average prestige scores of college graduates are 41.8 for whites and 36.8 for blacks. So, blacks with more

---

[6] Wages change during the course of the first job. Only starting wages are used in this analysis, since wages at the end of the first job are very strongly influenced by its duration—wages increase with the length of the job.

TABLE 2.10   MEAN OCCUPATIONAL PRESTIGE AND STARTING WAGES OF FIRST JOB
AFTER ENTRY, BY EDUCATION AT ENTRY AND RACE

Education at Entry	Mean Occupational Prestige		Mean Starting Wages ($/month)	
	White	Black	White	Black
Less than 5 years	22.0	21.3	95	100
4-7 years	22.0	21.1	115	137
Elementary school graduate	23.1	21.9	167	174
Some high school	26.5	23.9	228	200
High school graduate	28.2	26.0	249	221
High school graduate and some vocational	29.1	28.8*	163*	277*
Some college	32.7	29.9	271	279
College graduate	41.8	36.8	321	297
Master's degree	52.1	78.3*	512	250*
Some graduate or professional	53.9*	-	350*	-
Graduate or professional degree	61.8	-	361	-
Total	29.3	24.8	243	200
Number of cases	844	736	618	526
Percent of variance explained by education	31.6	17.7	19.1	13.6
Missing values (percent) In armed forces			16.8	16.3
Other	.7	.3	10.5	12.5
Total number of cases	850	738	850	738

*   Less than 5 cases

education are *relatively* worse off than those with less schooling. The class effects observed, at least insofar as they are measured by education, are much larger than those due to race. Looking at later occupational achievement, Blau and Duncan (1967:208) also find that the socioeconomic difference between races grows with increasing education.

An analysis of variance reveals that educational attainment at entry
explains 31.6% of the variance in the first job prestige score for whites and
only 17.7% for blacks. Thus the "transformation" of education into job
quality is less certain for blacks than for whites, as was the conversion of
family background into education. The lower prestige scores of blacks
arise from two sources: Blacks have less education, and they obtain poorer
jobs than whites with comparable levels of schooling. To measure the
relative magnitudes of these two effects, the first job occupational prestige score is regressed on the respondents' educational attainment at entry
and race. Ten dummy variables are used to represent educational attainment, thus avoiding any assumption of linearity in the relationship between prestige and education; race is measured by a single dummy variable. Individual cases are weighted so that the impact of the black sample
is adjusted to the actual proportion of blacks in the corresponding age
cohort in the American population,[7] so that the regression generates
estimates for the population as a whole. This regression is presented in
Table 2.11.

Race and education together explain 31.6% of the variance in the
first job prestige score. With education held constant, the difference in the
mean prestige scores of blacks and whites falls from 4.5 to 2.2 prestige
points, the value of the regression coefficient for race. So, approximately
one-half of the difference between white and black prestige scores disappears when the educational difference is removed. Relative to the group of
men with less than 4 years of schooling, a high school diploma is worth 5.8
prestige points, and a college degree 19.3 prestige points. The unique
variance explained by the race variable is only 0.3%, the unique effect of
education is 30.2%, and 1.1% of the variance is "shared"[8] by the two
factors—to give the total explained variance of 31.6%. It is important to
note that the low variance attributed to race reflects the fact that only a
small part of the population is black, which limits the importance of the

[7] In the American population, 11.4% of the men between ages 30 and 39 in
1968—the time of the interview—were blacks (see U.S. Bureau of the Census,
1970b:212).
[8] The sum of the unique effects of all the independent variables (or groups of
variables) is almost always less than the total variation explained by all of the
variables together. This remainder cannot be allocated to any one (or group of)
independent variable(s). It is shared among, or common to, the variables taken
together. The difference is caused by multicolinearity among the independent variables.

TABLE 2.11   REGRESSION OF OCCUPATIONAL PRESTIGE AND STARTING WAGES
             OF FIRST JOB AFTER ENTRY ON RACE AND EDUCATION AT
             ENTRY

Independent Variable or Group of Variables	Dependent Variable	
	Occupational Prestige of First Job	Starting Wages of First Job ($/month)
REGRESSION COEFFICIENTS		
Race†	-2.2	-16*
Education at entry†		
5-7 years	0.0*	22*
Elementary school graduate	0.8*	67*
Some high school	4.0	124
High school graduate	5.8	146
High school graduate and some vocational	6.9*	76*
Some college	10.2	171
College graduate	19.3	219
Master's degree	30.1	406
Some graduate or professional	31.5	247
Ph.D. or professional degree	39.5	258
Regression constant	22.4	102
PERCENT OF VARIANCE EXPLAINED		
Zero-order effect		
Race	1.4	.9
Education at entry	31.3	19.0
Unique effect		
Race	.3	.1
Education at entry	30.2	18.1
Common	1.1	.8
Total without interaction	31.6	19.0
Interaction effect	.1	.3
Total with interaction	31.7	19.3

* Not statistically significant at .05
† Effects measured relative to whites, with no high school

race variable. The insertion of ten dummy variables to measure the interaction of race and education adds only .1% to the total variance.

Even in 1959 dollars, the starting wages of these first jobs after entry into the labor force are very low (see Table 2.10). Whites with less than 5 years schooling earn an average of only $95 per month, while the mean for blacks is $100 per month; for white and black high school graduates the averages are $228 and $200 per month; and for college graduates they are $321 and $297 per month. There is a quite uniform increase in wages with rising education, unlike the curvilinear relationship found for prestige. As education increases, there is a significant reversal in the position of whites and blacks. Among the men with no high school, blacks have *higher* wages (the difference is greatest for those with between 5 and 7 years of schooling, for whom it amounts to $22 per month). However, for individuals with at least some high school, whites are generally paid more than blacks with the same education, with a few exceptions. Blacks with higher levels of education are relatively worse off, as we found in our consideration of first job prestige scores, but the differences for wages are not so large.

Educational attainment (again in eleven categories) explains 19.1% of the variance in first job wages for white and 13.6% for blacks. Thus, education is a far better predictor of occupational prestige than of wages, and again it is easier to predict the wages of whites than those of blacks. The difference between the means of white and black wages amounts to $43 per month. Following the procedure for the prestige variable, the starting wage of the first job is then regressed on education at entry and race. A high school diploma is found to be "worth" $146 per month (over the lowest category—less than 5 years schooling), and a college diploma, $219 per month (again in comparison to men with no high school). The net effect of race, with education removed, amounts to $16 per month. Thus the wage deficit is reduced by over 60% with education held constant. Only .1% of the variance in the first job wage is uniquely attributable to race, 18.1% is due to education and .8% cannot be uniquely assigned to either factor. The race variable has a stronger effect on prestige scores than on wages. As in the prestige analysis, the interaction between education and race is very small; the ten interaction variables add only .3% to the explained variance.

Finally, let us examine the relationship between the prestige score and wages of the first job. It is rather weak. The simple correlations between the two measures are .316 for whites and .215 for blacks, yielding explained variances of 10.0% and 4.6% respectively. Thus the relationship between occupational prestige and wages is not nearly so large as that between either of them and education. Much of the prestige—wage correlation can be explained by education. Their partial correlations, holding education constant, are only .142 for whites and .102 for blacks, for which the explained variances are 2.0% and 1.0%! This is an important finding, for the fact that the two occupational dimensions are only weakly related suggests that mobility in one of the directions, say increasing wages, has no necessary connection to higher prestige scores. Though no exactly comparable data are available, Duncan, Featherman, and Duncan (1972:38) report corresponding values for jobs held later in the careers of native whites. They obtain a value of .337 for the socioeconomic status—income correlation, which drops to .248 (by our calculation) when education is held constant, for their 25—34 year age cohort; the corresponding partial correlations are .442 and .282 for the 35—44 year cohort. These higher values suggest that the two variables become more strongly attached later in men's careers. Chapter 5 examines this relationship at a later stage in our respondents' careers.

Features of the First Job

This section describes the way in which men enter the labor force and relates it to their levels of educational attainment and race. The five variables treated describe the process of getting the job (including the extent of unemployment), the marital status of the respondent, whether he moved and the distance of such a move, and how he located the first job, and the job itself (whether it was in the armed forces or the civilian labor force, and, if the latter, the industry in which the job was classified).

1. *Unemployment before the First Job.* Most respondents are able to find their first jobs very rapidly—66% of the whites and 65% of the blacks are at their first jobs within the month following the one in which they enter the labor force. Since our survey uses 1 month as the finest unit of time, it permits only a relatively crude measure of unemployment— periods of unemployment lasting up to 7 weeks can escape detection entirely. Among the men with no high school, whites experience somewhat more unemployment than blacks; but with increasing education, it is

TABLE 2.12   DURATION OF UNEMPLOYMENT BEFORE FIRST JOB BY EDUCATION
AT ENTRY AND RACE

Race and Education at Entry	Unemployment before First Job (in months) Percentage Distribution				Mean	Number of cases
	Less Than 1*	1-6	More Than 6	Total		
White						
No high school	58	17	25	100	5.9	132
Some high school	70	17	13	100	3.5	179
High school graduate	64	29	7	100	1.6	365
Some college	82	14	4	100	0.8	83
College graduate	64	29	7	100	2.0	91
Total	66	23	11	100	2.6	850
Black						
No high school	63	15	22	100	5.6	184
Some high school	71	11	18	100	4.0	260
High school graduate	59	34	7	100	2.3	221
Some college	77	12	11	100	4.5	48
College graduate	36	52	12	100	3.3	25
Total	65	20	15	100	3.9	738

*Due to the form of the questionnaire, any unemployment of respondents who obtained their first jobs in the same month as they entered the labor force or who entered the labor force in one month and found a job in the next month was not recorded; all such individuals are placed in this first category.

clear that blacks have more difficulty finding jobs (see Table 2.12). For example, 64% of white college graduates locate their first jobs within a month of entering the labor force, compared to 36% of black college graduates. Thus, blacks with less education appear to be *relatively* (compared to whites) better off than those with more! The labor market thus discriminates against well-educated blacks, though it is easy for those with little education to find first jobs.

Though this finding is based on very small numbers of cases, particularly for the highly educated black groups, some of the Bureau of Labor Statistics surveys provide support for it. Hamel (1966:A5) finds the unemployment rates (in October 1965) of high school *graduates* of the previous spring are 10.8% for whites and 26.9% for non-whites. For high school *dropouts* of the same age cohort, the rates are 20.3% for whites and 20.0% for non-whites.[9] Three later studies show evidence of this pattern (O'Boyle 1968:A6, A7, A11; Hayghe 1970:A7, A8; Young 1973:A19), but others report contrary results (Perrella 1969:A6; Hayghe 1972:A9, A10; Michelotti 1974:A19). This suggests that the unemployment rates of particular groups of young workers are very volatile, but that our findings of a particular pattern of racial and educational differences in unemployment, for the cohort which entered the labor force between the end of the war and 1960, are not unreasonable.

Kohen and Parnes (1971:42) also report some comparable results when they examine the mean number of weeks of unemployment for a sample of youths between the ages of 14 and 24. They find that blacks experience more unemployment at all levels of education but that the largest racial differences are at the highest levels of education. Among men with no high school, Kohen and Parnes find the mean period of unemployment is 2.1 weeks for whites, 2.7 weeks for blacks; for high school graduates the figures are .8 weeks and 1.7 weeks; and for men with at least some college, they are .5 and 1.6 weeks.

2. *Marital Status.* Few men are married when they enter the labor force (see Table 2.13). We find that while men who enter with high school diplomas are generally older, by an average of 1.3 years, than those who enter with only some high school, yet 5.4% of the blacks with some high school are married at the start of the first job, compared to only 1.8% of the graduates. The same pattern is found for whites, though the difference is much smaller. Again, for blacks, 14.6% of those with some college are married when they start their first job, compared to 12.0% of college graduates, even though the college graduates average 2 years older. Early marriage is clearly associated with the decision of some men to drop out of school and get a job. The proportion of men who were married increases only slightly in the very short interval between entry and the start of the first job.

3. *Geographic Moves.* About one-tenth of respondents move in the period between entry and the start of their first jobs—a move being defined as covering a distance of 10 miles or more and *not* within the same city. A very slightly greater proportion of blacks than whites move, but

[9] The calculation of the unemployment rate for black dropouts is mine, and is based on a very small number of cases.

TABLE 2.13   PROPORTIONS OF MEN WHO MOVED BETWEEN ENTRY AND THE START OF THEIR FIRST JOB AND THE PROPORTIONS MARRIED AT ENTRY AND AT THE START OF THEIR FIRST JOBS AFTER ENTRY, BY EDUCATION AT ENTRY AND RACE

Education at Entry	Percent Married at Entry		Percent Married at Start of First Job		Percent Who Moved		Number of Cases	
	White	Black	White	Black	White	Black	White	Black
No high school	0	1	1	1	14	10	132	184
Some high school	2	4	3	5	4	8	179	260
High school graduate	2	2	2	2	6	13	365	221
Some college	6	10	6	15	8	13	83	48
College graduate	26	8	27	12	26	24	91	25
Total	4.6	3.0	5.2	3.8	9.2	10.3	850	738

TABLE 2.14   METHOD OF LOCATING THE FIRST JOB, BY EDUCATION AT ENTRY AND RACE

Race and Education at Entry	Percentage Distribution								Missing Values (percent of all cases)	Number of cases
	Friends	Family	Public Agency	Private Agency	Advertisement	Direct Application	Promotion	Total		
White										
No high school	25	46	2	0	2	25	0	100	9	125
Some high school	28	29	2	2	5	33	1	100	12	136
High school graduate	25	30	4	2	6	32	1	100	11	310
Some college	10	32	2	2	8	42	4	100	12	59
College Graduate	15	17	3	8	3	54	0	100	13	76
Total	23	31	3	2	5	34	1	100	11	706
Black										
No high school	22	52	1	1	1	23	26	100	13	183
Some high school	38	25	2	0	2	32	36	100	11	205
High school graduate	28	24	5	1	7	34	47	100	8	180
Some college	32	16	3	6	3	43	49	100	6	33
College graduate	6	12	12	6	0	64	82	100	6	18
Total	29	31	3	1	3	32	1	100	10	619

the difference is insignificant—10% compared to 9%. The relationship of education to the probability of moving is very unsystematic, except that college graduates, one in four of whom move, are more likely to move than any of the four groups with lower levels of education. With respondents' education held constant, men who move during the entry period experience more unemployment in this interval—an average of 3.3 extra months for whites and 6.8 months for blacks. This suggests that difficulty in finding jobs is associated with moving, though unfortunately the causal ordering of the two variables is not clear. Zeller *et al.* (1970:52) find a reasonably similar relationship between migration and education.

The average distance of these moves is 411 miles for whites and 391 miles for blacks; the standard deviations are 523 miles for whites and 296 miles for blacks.[10] Among the individuals who move (78 whites and 76 blacks), the distance of the move is positively correlated with the starting wage of the first job but bears no relationship to the prestige score of that job. Holding education constant, whites gain $1 per month in salary for each 9.7 miles moved, while blacks gain $1 for each 10.5 miles moved. This finding seems reasonable. A move does not give a man the new skills that would enable him to obtain a different kind of job, but it certainly can get him higher pay for doing the same thing.

4. *Method of Locating the Job.* Respondents were asked to describe how they found their first jobs, and their responses were classified into seven categories: through a family member, through friends, through public and private employment agencies, through advertisements, by direct application, and by promotion. The data were also reaggregated into three categories: jobs found by personal contact, through family or friends, labeled "personal"; those found through promotion; and all the remaining groups which include first jobs found on the initiative of the job seeker, labeled "direct". The distributions are in Table 2.14.

Men with more education tend to use "direct" methods of finding jobs and are correspondingly less likely to rely on the contacts of friends and family. For whites, 71% of the men who did not attend high school use "personal" methods to get the first job, compared to 55% of the high school graduates and only 32% of the college graduates. For blacks, the corresponding proportions are 74%, 52%, and 18%. Within the "personal"

---

[10] The distances of the moves were calculated by geocoding every location mentioned by the respondents with its longitude and latitude, a simple trigonometric function was then used to measure the distance between any two locations.

category, the reliance shifts, with increasing education, from family to friends. As education increases, more men obtain their first jobs through direct application; about one-quarter of the respondents with no high school do so, compared to about 60% of college graduates. Private and public agencies and advertisements are only rarely used to find jobs. Bradshaw (1973:37) and Parnes et al. (1970:101) obtain relatively similar results.

5. *Industry of the First Job, Including Military Service.* One in six men have their first jobs in the armed forces. Though very nearly equal proportions of blacks and whites enter military service, there is a greater tendency for poorly educated whites than blacks to do so; however, at the higher levels of education, blacks are more likely to join (see Table 2.15). This pattern appears to work to the disadvantage of blacks. For men with little schooling, joining the armed forces represent a chance to obtain skills and education (usually equivalent to high school graduation) that they are unlikely to find in a civilian job. Of white college graduates, 16.4% enter the military, compared to 28.0% for blacks (the proportions are significantly different at .05). But for these men, the jobs in the armed forces are considerably poorer than those they might expect to find in civilian life (leaving aside the risks of death or injury in time of war). This may reflect the difficulty experienced by well-educated blacks in finding good civilian jobs. The young age at which men with little education enter the labor force bars them from military service; however, since the age distributions are very similar for blacks and whites of the same education, this should have no impact on the comparative rates of entry into military service.

The relatively small size of the sample makes a full analysis of the industry of the first job impossible. Based on the first digit of the Census industrial code, the 211 major industries are classified into six categories: Agriculture, forestry, fisheries, and mining (together with construction) are placed in a single category; the occupations in finance, insurance, and real estate are combined with public administration in one category; the remaining four categories are manufacturing, transportation, wholesale and retail trade (labeled "trade"), and services of all kinds (see U.S. Bureau of the Census 1970a). Such a gross classification necessarily obscures the relationship of industry to other variables, but a rough classification is necessary if the variable is to be treated at all.[11]

---

[11] After much of the analysis had been completed we realized that placing the construction industry in with agriculture and other primary industries made it

TABLE 2.15 INDUSTRY OF FIRST JOB AFTER ENTRY BY EDUCATION AT ENTRY AND RACE

Race and Education at Entry	Percentage Distribution								Number of cases
	Military Service	Primary & Constr.	Manufact- uring	Trans- port	Trade	Finance & Public Admin.	Service	Total	
Whites									
No high school	5	57	.17	2	13	1	10	100	132
Some high school	25	28	33	9	21	1	8	100	179
High school graduate	15	31	27	9	23	3	7	100	365
Some college	29	20	36	12	22	3	7	100	83
College graduate	16	12	24	6	8	8	42	100	91
Total	17	32	27	8	19	3	11	100	850
Blacks									
No high school	1	58	19	1	14	1	7	100	184
Some high school	22	33	25	5	22	1	14	100	260
High school graduate	19	17	36	2	26	5	14	100	221
Some college	31	9	40	3	18	6	24	100	48
College graduate	28	6	11	6	11	16	50	100	25
Total	17	34	26	3	20	3	14	100	738

Of the respondents whose first jobs are in the civilian labor force, about one-third find jobs in the primary industry and construction category, just over one-quarter go into manufacturing jobs, one-fifth are in wholesale and retail trades, about one-tenth are in services, and just less than 3% are in finance and public administration. The only important difference between the distributions of whites and blacks is in the transportation industry, which employs 7% of the whites but only 3% of the blacks. The industry in which a man finds his first job is strongly influenced by his educational attainment. The number of men whose first jobs are in primary industry and construction falls sharply with increasing education. Almost six in ten whites with no high school are in this category, compared to three-tenths of white high school graduates and one-tenth of white college graduates. The manufacturing industry and wholesale and retail trades draw many workers from the middle levels of education and fewer poorly educated or well-educated men. The service industry employs about one-half of all college graduates but a far smaller proportion of men at all of the lower levels of education. No really comparable data on the industry of first jobs of this cohort is available, though Parnes *et al.* (1970:86–88) and the Bureau of Labor Statistics studies of high school graduates (e.g., Hamel 1966:A10; Perrella 1969:A10; Young 1973:A14; etc.) have more recent data.

MULTIVARIATE ANALYSIS OF THE QUALITY OF THE FIRST JOB

Finally, taking the variables describing the entry process and those relating to family background, pre-entry work experience, and education, we analyze their relative effects on the occupational prestige and wages of the first job. The fact that the variables described above vary according to

---

difficult to compare our results with those of other researchers, and that it obscured an interesting aspect of occupational mobility. The logic of our classification was that the two major industries, which consist primarily of blue collar jobs outside of manufacturing, should be placed in the same category. We should note that there are really not enough cases to carry out a full analysis of industrial transitions and that the main focus is on prestige and wage mobility. Approximately one half of the 32% of whites and the 34% of blacks in the "primary industry and construction" category have first jobs in agriculture.

race and education is no guarantee that they affect the levels of these jobs. The prestige regression is based on all the cases, including men whose first jobs are in the armed forces (which are ranked like any other jobs on the occupational scale). The wage regression omits those men whose first jobs are in the armed forces, since their rates of pay are not comparable to those in the civilian labor force. The wage regression does not include the prestige among the independent variables, since the two dimensions of job quality appear to be quite unrelated at this early stage in men's careers. Again, separate regressions are carried out for whites and blacks. We proceed by first describing the variables used, then present the prestige and wage results, and conclude with a discussion of the racial differences and causal ordering of the variables. The means and summary descriptions of all the variables are in Table 2.16.

Family background is again measured by four variables, and the number of full-time and of part-time pre-entry jobs is also entered in the regression. Educational attainment of the respondent is measured with four dummy variables, splitting it into the five main categories. Educational attainment of each respondent's parents is measured on the 10-point scale described above. This method of representing the effect of education explains almost exactly the same amount of variation as do the dummy variables.[12] Our interest in the form of the relationship of respondent's education to prestige and wage values leads us to use the four dummy variables in this case. It was possible to use a larger number of dummy variables and hence to more accurately represent education at entry, but this would have suggested the respondent's education was far more precisely measured than the other two education variables and might have exaggerated the impact of this variable.

Eleven variables describe the nature of the first job and of the entry process. A single dummy variable measures the impact of entering the armed forces as a first job—it is not included in the wage regressions since they are based only on respondents with civilian first jobs. Military service, as defined here, is an industry—so we can compare military jobs to those in

---

[12] When the occupational prestige of the first job after entry of whites was regressed on educational attainment measured in three different ways, the results were as follows: An 11-category analysis of variance (identical to a regression with ten dummy variables) explains 31.6% of the variation in the prestige scores; a five category analysis of variance (using the four dummy variables in the large regressions in Tables 12 and 13) explains 27.6%; and a linear regression, using the 10-point scale, explains 27.0%.

TABLE 2.16   VARIABLES USED IN REGRESSION ANALYSIS OF OCCUPATIONAL PRESTIGE
AND STARTING WAGES OF FIRST JOB AFTER ENTRY

Variable	White	Black	Comments
	Mean or Proportion		
Family background			
Father's education	2.04	1.66	Education is measured on the ten-
Mother's education	2.79	2.16	point scale, in Table 2.1
Father's occupation	36.1	28.2	
Number of siblings	3.64	5.35	
Education at entry			Four dummy variables, so no as-
Some high school	.211	.352	sumption of linearity is necessary;
High school graduate	.429	.300	each effect is measured relative
Some college	.098	.065	to the lowest group with no high
College graduate	.107	.034	school, not relative to the previous group
Number of jobs before entry			
Full-time	1.31	.40	
Part-time	1.13	.47	
First Job			
Geographic move*	.092	.103	Dummy variable with the value one
Distance of move*	38.1	42.4	for men who moved ten miles or more, not within a city; in miles, zero for men who did not move
Marital status	.052	.039	Dummy variable with the value one for men married at the start of the first job
Method of locating job*			Two dummy variables; effects
Direct	.440	.389	measured relative to the group
Promotion	.010	.005	who located their first jobs through family or friends
Industry			Six dummy variables; effects
Military service*	.168	.161	measured relative to the group in
Manufacturing	.221	.222	the primary industries and con-
Transportation	.065	.023	struction; no military service
Trade	.161	.171	variable is included in the wage
Finance and public			regressions since they exclude
administration	.024	.022	men with first jobs in the armed
Service	.093	.115	forces
Occupational prestige of first job	29.3	24.8	
Starting wages of first job	243	200	In $/month; dollars price adjusted to 1959 values

* Not defined for men with first jobs in the armed forces

civilian industries. Another dummy variable measures the impact of a move by the respondent (10 miles or more and not within the same city) between entry and the start of his first job. The distance of this move, which is given the value of zero when there is no move, is also included in the regression.

The method of finding the first job is classified into three categories: personal (using family and friends), direct (private and public agencies, advertisement, direct application), and by promotion. The differences between the last two of these categories, direct and promotion, and the personal category are measured by two dummy variables. Another dummy variable measures the difference between men who are married and those who are not at the start of their first job. Last, a group of five dummy variables shows the differences between jobs in five specific industries and those in the category that includes the primary industries and construction.

The use of multiple regression requires some strong assumptions, particularly that the distributions of the variables will not differ too markedly from normality, and that the effects of these variables are additive and not the result of interaction. Bohrnstedt and Carter (1971) argue that the regression procedure is very robust in the absence of large measurement errors. Though it is almost impossible to test all of the possible interactions among these variables, an examination of the relationships between education attainment and each of the variables describing the first job did not reveal any very large interaction effects.[13] The prestige regression is in Table 2.17, the wage regression in Table 2.18, and Table 2.19 contains a summary of the variances accounted for by each of the four groups of variables.

The Prestige Regression

The twenty-one variables in Table 2.17 explain 38.8% of the variation in the first job prestige score for whites, and rather less, 28.7%, for

---

[13] A typical example showing the extent of the interaction is as follows: Respondent's educational attainment and the industry of his first job, measured by nine dummy variables in all, explained 18.8% of the variation in the wage of the first job. The addition of twenty interaction variables (all dummy variables) raises the explained variance by 3.5% to 22.3%. So, there is some interaction, but the main effects are responsible for the greatest part of the total explained variance.

TABLE 2.17   REGRESSION OF OCCUPATIONAL PRESTIGE OF FIRST JOB AFTER ENTRY ON
             FAMILY BACKGROUND, EDUCATION AT ENTRY, NUMBER OF JOBS BEFORE
             ENTRY AND CHARACTERISTICS OF THE JOB BY RACE

Independent Variable	Regression Coefficient		Standardized Regression Coefficient		Correlation with Dependent Variable	
	White	Black	White	Black	White	Black
Family background						
Father's education	-.22	.45	-.036	.081	.211	.282
Mother's education	.27	-.15	.037	-.025	.248	.232
Father's occupation	-.037	.102	.038	.135*	.230	.261
Number of siblings	-.14	.05	-.033	.020	-.176	-.114
Education at entry						
Some high school	1.8	.6	.061	.032	-.122	.003
High school graduate	3.4	3.4	.139*	.101†	-.079	.125
Some college	7.3	4.5	.180*	.125*	.091	.159
College graduate	17.9	12.0	.463*	.244*	.479	.147
Number of jobs before entry						
Full-time	-.63	-.34	-.113*	-.048	.268	.037
Part-time	.52	-.40	.079†	-.051	.255	.094
First Job						
Geographic move	1.5	-1.2	.035	-.042	.165	.017
Distance of move	.0035	.0018	.098	.034	.120	.044
Marital status	.5	-2.0	.009	-.044	.200	.019
Method of locating job						
Direct	2.3	1.3	.094*	.072†	.218	.135
Promotion	11.4	2.4	.092*	.020	.061	.064
Industry						
Military service	5.1	6.9	.158*	.283*	.027	.257
Manufacturing	4.6	2.0	.161*	.095	.050	-.028
Transportation	6.6	.6	.136*	.010	.067	-.042
Trade	2.9	1.1	.090	.046	-.133	-.093
Finance & public administration	10.6	10.8	.134*	.176*	-.002	.181
Service	11.4	5.7	.275*	.203*	.039	.184
Regression constant	18.6*	11.0*				

† Statistically significant at .05
* Statistically significant at .01

blacks. When first job prestige is regressed on the four variables measuring family background *alone*, they account for 9.0% of the variance for whites and 10.5% for blacks. Their unique effects—the variance explained after all the other variables had been entered in the regression—amount to only 0.3% for whites and 2.7% for blacks. Hence, almost all of the impact of family background is indirect, it flows through other variables, primarily the respondent's education. None of the family background variables has a statistically significant effect for whites. For blacks, each 10 points of father's occupational prestige adds 1 prestige point to son's job, and each 1 point of father's education adds 0.5 prestige points to the son's job, but number of siblings and mother's education have no significant impact.

Level of educational attainment, even when all other factors are held constant, remains a major influence on the first job—the four dummy variables uniquely explain 8.4% of the variance for whites and 5.0% for blacks. Still, when education *alone* is used to predict prestige, the variances are very much larger—32.6% for whites and 16.4% for blacks. So, the greater part of the effect of education cannot be separated from that of other variables, as for example when education influences the industry of the first job, which in turn affects its prestige value. The regression confirms our earlier observation of the curvilinear relationship of education to prestige and the finding that the racial differences in the value of each unit of education increase at higher levels of education. A high school diploma is worth 3.4 prestige points to a white respondent, 2.0 to a black; some college is worth 7.3 points to a white respondent, 4.5 to a black; and a college degree adds 17.9 points for whites, 12.0 for blacks (all of these results are measured from the lowest category of education, no high school).

By comparing the values of these regression coefficients to the absolute differences in the prestige scores of men at the five levels of education, it is possible to examine the extent to which the controls on all the other variables reduce the impact of education. For example, the difference in the mean prestige scores of whites with no high school and high school graduates is 5.6 points, but the corresponding regression coefficient is 3.4 points. For black high-school graduates the raw difference is 4.7 points, but the regression coefficient is only 2.0 points. Similarly, the value of a college degree (over a high school diploma) is reduced from 13.3 to 10.6 prestige points for whites, from 8.6 to 7.5 for blacks. So, a larger part of the effect of lower levels of education is

mediated by other variables, while the impact of a college degree appears
to act very directly on job prestige.

The relationship between number of full-time and part-time jobs
before entry and the first job prestige score differs markedly at the
zero-order level between the two races, but these jobs have little direct
effect in either case. For whites, the simple correlation between number of
full-time jobs and education is .268, and between number of part-time jobs
and education it is .225. Together they explain 9.8% of the variance in the
first job prestige score, but in the regression, their unique effect is only
0.1%. The number of full-time jobs before entry is *negatively* related, to the
prestige value of the first job, though it has little impact; the number
of part-time jobs has a small positive effect. So, jobs held before entry do
not significantly enhance later occupational achievement. For blacks the
number of these jobs bears almost no relation to first job prestige at the
zero-order level; both the correlation coefficients are below .05, though
positive. With all the other variables held constant, there is a weak (their
combined effect is just short of significance at .05) *negative* association
between number of full-time and part-time jobs and the first job prestige
score. So, again, the implication is that blacks, to a greater extent than
whites, hold jobs before entry because of need—but any such difference is
not large enough to have much effect on later careers.

Marital status, geographic moves, and the distance of moves have
very little influence on first job prestige score. Married blacks have slightly
lower scores than single blacks, but there is no difference for whites.
Whites who move have slightly better first jobs, while there is a small
negative effect for blacks. In both cases, longer moves result in small
prestige gains. None of these effects reaches statistical significance, so we
will not speculate on their meaning.

Jobs located by "direct" methods have prestige scores averaging 2.3
points above those found with the aid of friends or family for whites, the
jobs into which men were promoted average 11.4 points more than jobs
found by personal contacts. The corresponding effects were weaker for
blacks, amounting to 1.3 and 2.4 prestige points respectively. However,
the estimates obtained for promotion are unreliable because of the very
small numbers of men who were promoted into these first jobs (which
required them to have held a job with the same firm, in either a full-time
or a part-time capacity, *before* entering the labor force). There is a real
payoff to going out and seeking a job, instead of relying on personal

contacts. Though, Table 2.14 shows, it is a benefit disproportionately concentrated among men with higher levels of education; those with little schooling tend to rely on people they know when seeking employment.

The six dummy variables describing the industry of the first job and whether it is in the armed forces have a strong effect on the prestige score of this job, they uniquely explain 7.5% of the variance for whites and 7.7% for blacks. This makes sense, since these variables are a very direct measure of the nature of that first job. Still, a great deal of the variation produced by these variables can be attributed to differences in the industry that are caused by the effects of educational attainment and other variables. These six industry variables alone account for 33.1% of the variance in prestige scores for whites and 26.9% for blacks—though, when jobs in the armed forces are excluded, these values are much smaller—they drop to 19.4% and 12.7% respectively.[14]

First jobs in the armed forces are, for whites, close to the average of the other industries; they have a regression coefficient of 5.1 points; but for blacks the estimate is 6.9 points, placing military jobs near the top of the six civilian industrial categories. So, holding respondent's education and family background and all other variables constant, it is clear that jobs in the armed forces are relatively more attractive to blacks. Since all of the industry dummy variables have positive effects, jobs in the primary industries and construction clearly rank at the bottom. The main racial difference in the ranking of the industries is that the range of effects is rather larger for whites. For blacks, jobs in the primary industries and construction, and in manufacturing, transportation and trade have quite similar prestige scores, service jobs are better, and those in finance and public administration are at the top. For whites, jobs in the primary industries and construction are clearly lowest, those in manufacturing, transportation, and trade are in the middle, and the service and finance and public administration categories rank highest.

To summarize, two groups of variables, measuring the respondent's education and the industry of this first job have strong direct and indirect effects on the prestige score of the job. Family background has a large indirect effect. The number of jobs before entry exerts a considerable

[14] Virtually all first jobs in the armed forces have the prestige score for the lowest rank of enlisted men—so there is almost no variation within this category. The score for this job in the armed forces is 30.0 points, about that of a factory operative.

indirect effect on prestige, but for whites only. The method used to locate
this job has a small direct effect, but the impact of marital status, and of
moving between entry and the start of the first job are negligible. Thus,
the determination of the prestige score of this first job is a complex
process in which five different groups of variables play some part.

The Wage Regression

The analysis of the starting wage of the first job differs from that of
the prestige regression only in that it is based on men whose first jobs are
not in the armed forces, so it excludes the dummy variable identifying
those jobs. As shown in Table 2.18, the twenty variables together explain
28.1% of the variation in the wages of whites, but just 15.3% for blacks.
So, there is a great deal more uncertainty in the wages of the first job for
blacks. These values are well below the corresponding variances in the
prestige analysis, for both blacks and whites.

The four family background variables *alone* explain 13.5% of the
variance in wages of the first job for whites and 3.9% for blacks—but their
unique variances are only 2.8% for whites and 0.7% for blacks. So, again,
the effect of family background is mediated through other variables at
later points in the chain connecting them to the first job. The respondent's
education at entry uniquely explains 2.1% of the variance in first job
wages for whites and 4.1% for blacks. These values are very much smaller
than the zero-order variances for education, which amount to 14.8% for
whites and 10.4% for blacks. The direct effect of education is comparatively greater for blacks, so the black regression coefficients, $112 per
month for a college degree and $59 per month for a high school diploma,
are a little larger than the corresponding values for whites—$98 and $51
per month, respectively.

The two variables measuring pre-entry work experience alone explain 12.9% of the variation in wages for whites, but only 1.1% for blacks.
With all the other variables inserted in the large regression, the explained
variances drop drastically, to 2.7% and 0.1% for whites and blacks,
respectively. So, the numbers of such jobs are also highly intercorrelated
with other variables in the equation, particularly education. For each
full-time job, whites gain an average of $5.9 per month, and for each
part-time job, $9.0 per month; for blacks, the corresponding values are

TABLE 2.18   REGRESSION OF STARTING WAGES OF FIRST JOB AFTER ENTRY ON FAMILY
BACKGROUND, EDUCATION AT ENTRY, NUMBER OF JOBS BEFORE ENTRY
AND CHARACTERISTICS OF THE JOB, BY RACE

Independent Variable	Regression Coefficient		Standardized Regression Coefficient		Correlation with Dependent Variable	
	White	Black	White	Black	White	Black
Family background						
Father's education	-3.2	5.9	-.044	.077	.202	.179
Mother's education	11.7	2.2	.143*	.027	.295	.174
Father's occupation	.76	-.58	.067	-.058	.217	.079
Number of siblings	-3.7	.3	-.080†	.010	-.221	-.066
Education two years after entry						
Some high school	48	42	.140*	.163*	-.052	.003
High school graduate	51	59	.186*	.222*	.044	.125
Some college	43	93	.087	.172*	.067	.159
College graduate	98	112	.223*	.156*	.288	.147
Number of jobs before entry						
Full-time	5.9	1.5	.093†	.015	.324	.050
Part-time	9.0	2.2	.124*	.020	.278	.106
First job						
Geographic move	1	-48	.001	-.128*	.138	.050
Distance of move	.119	.140	.174*	.186*	.181	.106
Marital status	1	42	.002	.069	.165	.137
Method of locating job						
Direct	14	14	.053	.056	.130	.134
Promotion	166	59	.119*	.036	.146	.064
Industry						
Manufacturing	15	9	.049	.033	.136	.138
Transportation	15	22	.029	.029	.067	-.027
Trade	-47	-19	-.138*	-.065	-.133	-.057
Finance & public administration	-38	81	-.046	.106*	-.002	.152
Service	-37	3	-.086*	.009	.039	.079
Regression constant	137	151				

* Statistically significant at .01
† Statistically significant at .05

positive but of negligible magnitude. So, while early job experiences have mostly negative effects on prestige scores, they do increase wages—earlier work experience does not help the respondent to find a different *kind* of job, at least insofar as it is measured on the prestige scale, but it increases the wages he can expect to be paid.

The ten remaining variables uniquely explain 7.6% of the variation in wages for whites, 4.0% for blacks—values which are about one-half the magnitude of the zero-order variances. Blacks who are married at the start of these jobs average $42 per month more in wages than those who are not, though their prestige scores are slightly *lower* than those of comparable single men. This suggests that married men trade prestige for wages, since wages are of greater concern to them. For whites, the marital status variable has no effect on either prestige or wages.

Moves prior to entry also have no effect on whites' wages, but cost blacks $48 per month in wages. The distance of the move significantly affects wages, to the extent of $12 per month for every 100 miles moved for whites, $14 per month for blacks. So, whites can expect higher wages from any move, but blacks must move more than 350 miles to make any gains. As noted above, it is reasonable that these moves should influence wages and not prestige scores, since a move allows an individual access to a different labor market but does not change the skills he possesses. Jobs that the respondent finds independently pay more than those located with the help of relatives or friends, by an average of $14 per month for men of either race. Those obtained by promotions (though we must again caution that the result is based on very few cases) are even better, paying for whites $166 per month and for blacks $59 per month above the jobs located by friends or relatives.

The industry of the first job has a great deal less impact on wages than on prestige scores. The pay differentials do not fall into any easily interpretable pattern. For whites, jobs in finance and public administration, which average over 10 prestige points *more* than jobs in the primary industries and construction, pay $40 per month *less* than the latter. Jobs in manufacturing and transportation pay between $10 and $20 above the primary group. Not only does the industry exert less than half the effect on wages that it does on job prestige, but the rank ordering of the six industrial categories varies markedly between the two variables. While the impact of the six industries on the prestige scores of whites and blacks is reasonably similar, there are marked racial differences in the impact of industry on the wages of this job.

The Importance of the Four Factors

In our discussion of the impact of the four clusters of variables, we have so far concentrated on their zero-order and unique effects. The result is that family background, which is the most separated in time from the first job, has very little impact, it explains no more than 3% of the variance in any case. For example, the unique effect of family background in the white prestige regression amounts to only .3% of the variance, compared to a zero-order effect of 9.0%. The difference of 8.7% is accounted for by the fact that family background has a strong effect on the respondent's education, and education in turn affects the prestige score. In path analysis terms, most of the effect of family background is indirect. The variation in prestige that is caused by family background raising the level of education may logically be attributed to family background, and *not* to education itself, which merely transmits this effect.

Following this argument, in order to discover the relative impact of the four groups of variables, we should compare the zero-order effect of family background to the *additional* variance explained by education, to the *additional* variance of pre-entry jobs (*after* family background and education have been included), and to the unique effect of the eleven variables describing the entry process (since they occur last in time). In Table 2.19 we contrast the unique variances to the values obtained in this way. The result is a radical change in the importance of the four factors. Taking the white prestige regression, not only is the 0.3% unique effect of family background replaced by a zero-order variance of 9.0%, but the impact of education rises from 8.4% to 19.3%, of pre-entry jobs from 1.0% to 1.1%, while the features of the first job that enter last explain 9.4% of the variance (their unique effect). Similar, though not quite so dramatic, results are obtained for the other regressions.

This procedure raises the variances of the variables that occur earliest in the causal sequence and lowers the variances of later variables. It also narrows the differences between the white and black variances, since the results are no longer so sensitive to the magnitudes of the intercorrelations among the independent variables. This method makes the following allocations for the prestige regression: family background, 9.0% for whites and 10.5% for blacks; education at entry, 19.3% for whites and 8.9% for blacks; pre-entry jobs, 1.1% for whites and 0.8% for blacks; characteristics of the entry process, 9.4% for whites and 8.5% for blacks. Thus, the main racial difference is due to educational attainment, which has only about

TABLE 2.19 PROPORTION OF VARIANCE EXPLAINED IN REGRESSION ANALYSES OF OCCUPATIONAL PRESTIGE AND STARTING WAGES OF FIRST JOB AFTER ENTRY, BY FOUR GROUPS OF VARIABLES, BY RACE

Dependent Variable and Group of Independent Variables	Percent of Variance Explained							
	White				Black			
	Zero-Order	Unique	Additional	Cumulative	Zero-Order	Unique	Additional	Cumulative
Occupational prestige of first job								
Family background	9.0	.3	9.0	9.0	10.5	2.7	10.5	10.5
Education at entry	27.6	8.4	19.3	28.3	14.7	5.0	8.9	19.4
Number of jobs before entry	9.8	1.0	1.1	29.4	14.2	5.6	.8	20.2
First job	25.2	9.4	9.4	38.8	19.6	8.5	8.5	28.7
Starting wages of first job								
Family background	11.5	2.8	11.5	11.5	3.8	.7	3.8	3.8
Education at entry	14.8	2.1	6.3	17.8	10.4	4.1	7.4	11.2
Number of jobs before entry	12.9	2.1	2.7	20.5	1.1	.1	.1	11.3
First job	12.3	7.6	7.6	28.1	8.8	4.0	4.0	15.3

half the impact on blacks' prestige scores that it has on whites'. Similarly, for the wage regression, the variance allocations for whites and blacks respectively are: 11.5% versus 3.8% for family background; 6.3% versus 7.4% for education; 2.7% versus 1.1% for pre-entry jobs; 7.6% versus 4.0% for the characteristics of the entry process. There are considerable differences for all of the groups of variables except education! Family background, in particular, has much less effect on black wages. So, the greater uncertainty in the black wage regression now takes on quite a different appearance—it appears as largely the result of family background and industry exerting less influence on black wages. It is hard to see how the greater variation of black wages within industries or the lower impact of family background on black wages is detrimental to blacks.

Allocation of the explained variance in a stepwise fashion according to the temporal order of the groups of variables separates the task of determining the relative importance of these variables from the form of the regression equation that best *predicts* the independent variable.

Finally, a comment on the unexplained variance in the prestige scores and wages of jobs is in order. Our most "successful" prediction, of white prestige scores, accounts for 38.8% of its variance, leaving 61.2% unexplained; the black wage regression accounts for only 15.3% of the variance, leaving 84.7% unexplained. We find prestige scores easier to predict than wages, and whites' jobs more predictable than blacks'. Though additional variables, or more accurate measures of the ones already included in the regression, would certainly bring about some increase in the explained variance, a radically different approach is necessary if they are to be increased substantially.

The implications of the racial difference are complex—on the one hand, black occupational achievement is less tied to education (in the case of prestige) and to family background (for wages), so blacks are less able to convert advantages in these variables into better jobs; on the other hand, blacks are less affected by their educational and background deficits than whites in their position would be. As Duncan (1968:95) argues, the prestige pattern is likely to work to the advantage of poorer blacks while hindering those with more education and from more privileged backgrounds. The lower wage variances suggest that the mechanisms of wage determination are rather different than those influencing prestige—situational factors, such as the wage rates within firms with new job openings, likely play a larger part in deciding wages.

Racial Differences

Let us examine once more the differences in the prestige scores and wages of whites and blacks and attempt to allocate them to different parts of the stratification process. Their mean prestige values differ by 4.5 points, and the insertion of the mean values of the dependent variables into the white regression reduces the deficit to 2.6 points, leaving a residual of 1.9 points that cannot be explained by family background, educational attainment, pre-entry work experiences, or the eleven other variables describing the first job. About 40% of the racial difference is removed by changing the prestige process for blacks and treating them like whites with equivalent characteristics. Now, if we were somehow to raise the background characteristics of blacks to those of whites while leaving the process alone, the gap would be narrowed from 4.5 to 1.9 points, the result obtained by substituting the white mean values in the black regression equation. Though this need not be the case—since an interaction between the forms of the regression equations and the differences of the mean values can take place—the effect of these two substitutions accounts for the entire racial difference of 4.5 prestige points.

Using Duncan's method (1968:101) it is possible to allocate the difference between the mean values of black and white prestige scores to the four groups of variables. Equalizing the family backgrounds of the two races alone would eliminate 2.5 of the 4.5 points difference—assuming that blacks are able to convert this increase into prestige at the same rate as whites. The equalization of both family background and education at entry would narrow the racial deficit to only .9 points; but the further equalization of the number of pre-entry jobs would increase the gap to 1.8 points, because of the negative relationship of the number of jobs to prestige, when family background and education are held constant. The equalization of all twenty-one variables would, as we noted above, result in a racial difference of 1.9 points. Thus, the most important roles in creating this difference appear to be played by family background and the residual "pure" discrimination. The impact of educational attainment, since a large part of its effect has been accounted for by the equalization of family background, is not so large, and it is counterbalanced by the negative effect of pre-entry jobs. The eleven variables in the "first job" group have no appreciable effect.

The result of applying these procedures to the $43 per month wage difference between blacks and whites is quite different. The substitution of the mean values of the independent variables for blacks into the white equation results in a predicted black wage $44 below the white average. So, the effect of race, once all the factors in the equation are removed, is very close to zero. Alternatively, the substitution of the white mean values in the black regression, equalizing the stratification processes, produces a racial difference of $22, and so eliminates half of the total gap. Here the results produced by the two forms of substitution do not conveniently add up to the total difference of $43.

Using Duncan's method the allocation of the $44 difference, obtained from the white regression, is $34 to family background, $1 to education, $1 to pre-entry jobs, and $7 to the other variables. Again, family background is the largest contributor and in this case it accounts for three-quarters of the total difference. The policy implications of this finding are rather discouraging, for the variables that are most difficult to change—parental education levels, father's occupation, and number of siblings—play a very important role in accounting for racial differences. The large, unaccounted-for portion of the prestige difference suggests that the barriers of discrimination play a more important role in deciding the type of job a black person will get than what he will get paid for doing it.

SUMMARY

This chapter presents a detailed description of entry into the labor force, up to the point at which men start their first jobs. A great many findings have emerged from the analysis, and its value may lie more in the richness of material than in any single startling result. The entry process appears to be a relatively rapid one—few men experience much unemployment before their first jobs. The quality of the first job is influenced mainly by family background, education, and the industry of the job, almost all of the effect of family background being transmitted through other variables, chiefly education at entry. Each of the four background variables has some independent effect on education. The inclusion of mother's education, in addition to the two variables usually used to describe the father (his education and occupation) significantly improves the model, particularly for blacks. Education and race shape the whole of the entry process, but some variables that they affect do not significantly influence the quality of the first job. Thus, while education and race both influence the method used to locate the first job, in itself this variable has only a very minor independent effect on prestige scores or wages. In a number of cases, we found readily interpretable effects that had little impact on the process as a whole. For example, married blacks do have higher wages than those who are single, but the difference is not large enough to be of much importance. A comparison of the wage and prestige regressions showed that the determination of these two separate aspects of the quality of the first job is quite independent.

The analysis of the numbers of jobs held before entry shows that they did fall into sensible patterns, as did their prestige scores and wages. While the fact that the numbers of jobs held increases with education and age at entry is perfectly predictable; what is more interesting is the finding that family background has almost no independent effect on their numbers—indeed there might be a small negative effect. Also, the large regressions reveal that these jobs have no appreciable impact on the quality of the first job after entry, except for a minor positive effect on the starting wages of whites. Pre-entry job experiences play an insignificant role in the determination of occupational achievement after entry, in spite of the fact that whites in general and men with more education have many more such jobs.

A detailed comparison of the experiences of whites and blacks up to the beginning of their first jobs after entry, reveals a pervasively discriminatory process. Blacks start out from poorer backgrounds, acquire less education, hold fewer and lower quality jobs before entry, and obtain first jobs with lower wages and prestige scores than whites. This process does not simply pass on initial inequalities of background, but adds to them at every step. So, for example, the racial differences in family background are not sufficient to explain all of the subsequent gap in educational attainment; nor are the differences in family background and education able to account for all of the differences in the numbers of jobs held before entry; and so on. Not all of the racial differences have a long-term impact. In particular, the fact that blacks get less work experience before entry has almost no effect on their first jobs. At some points there appear to be basic differences in the black and white stratification processes—for example, mother's education plays a much more important role in determining education for blacks. The extent of racial differences varies with educational attainment and according to the measure of job quality used. Blacks with more education appear to be the subject of more discrimination, and the prestige variable shows consistently larger racial differences than wages.

Trends in the Two Years after Entry

3

A significant shortcoming of our understanding of the entry process is that studies to date have told us relatively little about what happens to an individual after he obtains his first job. Once this job is known and the level of entry defined, interest shifts to later occupational achievement. This chapter describes the course of the first job and examines the jobs held at the points 1 and 2 years after entry. Again, the focus is on the relative positions of blacks and whites and of men with different levels of education. We will also be concerned with changes in the relationships between the prestige scores and wages of jobs, and family background, education, and jobs held before entry, as well as other variables, in order to determine the extent to which the stratification process itself changes in the first 2 yeas after entry. A path model of jobs held in this period is presented. The next chapter will deal with the impact of job mobility on an individual's standing *within* the group of men of equal education and of the same race, and with the factors beyond education and race that account for men changing jobs.

The rationale for treating the first job after entry and then the jobs held at the points 1 and 2 years after entry, and not the second, third, and later jobs, is straightforward. Even within categories of education attainment and race, the duration of the first job shows a great deal of variation; some respondents hold only one job in their entire careers (or at least until the point at which the interview takes place), while others hold many jobs in this period. So an analysis of the second job after entry would mean comparing, say, jobs held 6 months after entry to others that did not begin until the individual had been in the labor force for 10 years. By taking specific time points, 1 and 2 years after entry, it is possible to compare men who have spent equal amounts of time in the labor force, to hold constant the extent of occupational experience.

We do not deal with changes in educational attainment in the first 2 years after entry, since there is little educational mobility—less than 1% of the respondents gain significant amounts of education in this period. The reason for this stability lies in the definition of entry into the labor force that was decided upon—since, by that definition, a man enters the labor force only after discontinuing his full-time schooling for a period of 17 months (an academic year plus two summers) or more. The small number of changes that do occur result from part-time schooling, and they are far too infrequent to analyze.

MORE ABOUT THE FIRST JOB

Looking beyond the level of the first job, the characteristic of this job that has the greatest implications for the mobility process as a whole is its duration, for duration measures the role played by that first job in the context of a person's career. As shown in Table 3.1, white respondents spend an average of 24.9 months on the first job, compared to 34.7 months for blacks. One-fifth of the whites hold their first jobs for 4 months or less, and another one-fifth remain more than 3 years in the same first job. Only one-tenth of the blacks hold their first jobs for 4 months or less, and one-third of them remain more than 3 years. Individuals with the least education hold their first jobs for the longest time; for men with no high school, the mean duration is 34.7 months for whites and 46.4 months for blacks. Among white respondents, there is little difference in the mean durations of men in the four educational groups from "some high school" upward, though high school graduates have somewhat shorter durations than the other groups. In the black sample, men with some high school have significantly lower durations than high school graduates and those with further schooling. Within each category of educational attainment, blacks have longer first jobs than whites.

The skewed distribution of the duration variable means that mean durations are strongly influenced by a small number of very long first jobs.

TABLE 3.1 DURATION OF FIRST JOB AFTER ENTRY, BY EDUCATION AT ENTRY AND RACE

Race and Education at Entry	Duration of First Job after Entry (in months)					Mean	Number of Cases
	Percentage Distribution						
	1-4	4-12	13-36	37 or more	Total		
White							
No high school	13	30	32	35	100	34.7	132
Some high school	15	28	36	21	100	25.1	179
High school graduate	24	29	28	19	100	21.5	365
Some college	18	22	41	19	100	23.6	83
College graduate	27	20	23	19	100	25.2	91
Total	20	26	32	22	100	24.9	850
Black							
No high school	3	19	38	40	100	46.4	184
Some high school	8	19	40	33	100	35.4	260
High school graduate	15	21	36	28	100	26.9	221
Some college	13	20	38	29	100	26.6	48
College graduate	24	12	48	16	100	28.2	25
Total	10	19	38	33	100	34.7	738

However, there is a great deal of variation in the role played by this job within the whole career. A comparatively large number of respondents spend very little time at their first jobs, while for many others it represents a substantial portion of their total work experience. In one respect, the results are counterintuitive; blacks and the poorly educated are anything but "shiftless" or unsteady—instead, they are far *less* likely to change jobs than are whites and men with more education. The fact that lower durations are found among those respondents who, by such measures as education, prestige, and wages, are better off, suggests that job changes should be seen as steps up a career ladder and not as a sign of inability to settle down to work.

Though the patterns are unmistakable, the relationship between duration of first job and respondent's education is not very strong; when education is broken into 11 categories, it explains just 3.8% of the variation in the duration for whites and 4.7% for blacks. So, the *level* of this job, measured by its prestige score or wage rate, is far more predictable than its duration. Two more recent studies, by Zeller *et al.* (1970:28) and O'Boyle (1969), find that the job tenure of black workers is *shorter* than that of whites, holding age constant, but when education is held constant, they find no consistent racial differences among young workers. Both those surveys deal with the job held at the time of the interview, not with the first job. It is therefore impossible to say whether the job mobility of blacks has indeed increased since our data were collected or if the conflicting results might simply be an artifact of the differing measurements employed. Also, we include military service as a possible first job, whereas the Career Thresholds study and the Bureau of Labor Statistics surveys include only civilian jobs; however, the pattern of durations does not change if first jobs in the armed forces are excluded. Whatever the direction of the relationship, there is convincing evidence that job duration is only weakly related to race and educational attainment.

In the course of their first jobs our respondents receive three kinds of rewards, on-the-job training, promotion, and increased wages. As might be predicted, they are not equally distributed. Very few of the men, 8.9% of the whites and 3.7% of the blacks, obtain some training in the course of their jobs. Though the proportions of men receiving training are insufficient to allow a detailed analysis of the impact of education, it appears that men at the two lowest levels of education, those with no high school and those with some high school, have these opportunities less frequently

TABLE 3.2   PERCENT OBTAINING ON-THE-JOB TRAINING DURING FIRST
            JOB AFTER ENTRY, BY EDUCATION AT ENTRY, AND PERCENT
            PROMOTED AT THE END OF FIRST JOB, BY EDUCATION AT
            THE END OF FIRST JOB, BY RACE

Education at Entry	Some On-the-job Training (percent)		Promotion (percent)	
	White	Black	White	Black
No high school	5	3	5	3
Some high school	7*	1*	5	3
High school graduate	10	6	7*	3*
Some college	12	8	6	6
College graduate	11	4	7	4
Total	8.9	3.7	6.2*	3.3*

*   Black and white proportions differ at .05 (1 tail test)

than do those with more education. The results are shown in Table 3.2.
Also, within each educational category, whites are more likely to obtain
training than are blacks. On-the-job training is classified into 4 categories:
apprenticeship, formal management training, other formal training, and a
residual group labeled "informal and unspecified types." A comparison of
the numbers in each category again shows that blacks are disadvantaged.
Whites are twice as likely to hold apprenticeships (38% were apprentices
versus 15% of the blacks); one-half of the training experiences of whites
are of the "informal and unspecified" type compared to three-quarters of
those of blacks; about one-tenth of the training of both races is in the
remaining two categories.

Whites are also about twice as likely to be promoted; 6.2% are
promoted out of their first jobs, compared to 3.3% of the black workers.
There is only a weak positive association between the respondent's education and the probability of his being promoted. Again, the number of cases
is too small to present a full analysis. However, as was the case with
on-the-job training, there can be no doubt that the promotions accentuate

the educational and racial differences that are already in existence when the men entered the labor force. The differences are somewhat greater than might at first seem obvious because blacks and men with less education have longer first job durations—so the training and the promotions they do get take longer to occur.

Almost one-half of the respondents receive some wage increase during their first jobs, 45.1% of the whites and 48.9% of the blacks, as shown in Table 3.3. The average increase (among those receiving some increase) amounts to $75 per month for whites and $74 for blacks. There is no strong relationship between respondent's education and the likelihood of his receiving a wage increase, though individuals with some college appear more likely, and college graduates less likely, to get some raise, compared to the three lower educational groups. However, when we examine the average *size* of the increases, for those men who receive them, very large educational differences appear. The raises obtained by men with levels of education up to graduation from high school vary between $56 and $71, with blacks obtaining slightly greater increases; for those with some college the amounts are $94 for whites and $113 for blacks; for college graduates, the figures are $171 for whites and $173 for blacks (all in 1959 dollars per month). The net gains of the five education groups (i.e., the mean increase for the entire group, including those with some wage increase and those without any increase), display a similar pattern, favoring the best educated respondents.

The wage increase during the first job is rather weakly related to the variables that are strong predictors of the prestige score and starting wage of this job. For example, educational attainment explains only 1.2% of the variance in the wage increase for whites, and 2.9% for blacks. Its relationship to the industry of the first job, to the method by which the job is located, and to the variable measuring geographic moves before the first job are all statistically insignificant. But the respondent's marital status explains about 9% in the variance of the wage increase for blacks. This tallies with the earlier finding that married blacks have higher wages than unmarried blacks at the start of the first job.

The relationship between the wage at the start of the first job and the increase during that job is also very weak, the correlations between the two variables amount to .046 for whites and .146 for blacks; if prestige score is substituted for starting wage, correlations of .210 for whites and .151 for blacks are obtained. There is an important implication to all these

TABLE 3.3. PERCENT OBTAINING SOME WAGE INCREASE AND MEAN WAGE INCREASE DURING FIRST JOB, BY EDUCATION AT ENTRY AND RACE

Education at Entry	Percent with Some Wage Increase		Mean Wage Increase ($/Month)		For Men with Some Increase, Mean Wage Increase ($/Month)		Number of Cases	
	White	Black	White	Black	White	Black	White	Black
No high school	48	48	27	30	56	64	96	140
Some high school	52	48	32	39	62	71	122	175
High school graduate	42	49	28	33	67	68	276	169
Some college	56	66	53	74	94	113	55	29
College graduate	32	33	55	58	171	173	69	18
Total	45.1	48.9	34	36	75	74	618	526

weak results: The variables that serve as strong predictors of the level of the first job tell us very little about advancement within that job once it has begun.

1 AND 2 YEARS AFTER ENTRY

The mean increase in prestige scores during the first 2 years after entry is not large; as shown in Table 3.4, it amounts to 2.4 points for whites, and 1.2 points for blacks—values that should be seen in the context of distributions with standard deviations of the order of 10 points.[1] Though the magnitude of these increases is small, it is certainly significant that the gain for whites is twice as large as that for blacks. For the white sample there is little difference in the prestige gains made by men with various levels of education, except for those with the lowest level of education; for this group, those with no high school, prestige rises by only .4 points in the 2 years. For the black sample, the two lowest groups, those with no high school and those with some high school, make gains of only .2 and .6 points respectively. So the gap between the least educated men and the rest of the sample increases during this period.

The precise nature of the mobility that occurs is clearer in Table 3.5, where we tabulate the proportions of men in three prestige categories and in the armed forces, at entry and 1 and 2 years after entry. An examination of the high school graduates reveals these changes: a large decrease in the number of men in the very poorest jobs (prestige score under 20), a substantial decrease in the proportion with somewhat better jobs (ranked 20–29.9), no change in the number with scores of 30 or more, and a large increase in the number who are in the armed forces. So the overall shift is out of the very poorest and the relatively poor jobs into the armed forces. To a more limited extent, this kind of change also takes place among whites with some high school. However, there is very little mobility among

---

[1] Because there is considerable unemployment during this period, wages and occupational prestige scores of some respondents—those who held no jobs—are undefined at the points 1 and 2 years after entry. In these cases, in order to cut down the number of missing values, the jobs held closest to those points in time, and their prestige scores and wages, are substituted in the analysis.

TABLE 3.4   MEAN OCCUPATIONAL PRESTIGE OF THE FIRST JOB AFTER ENTRY
            AND ONE AND TWO YEARS AFTER ENTRY, BY EDUCATION AT THE
            TIME AND RACE

| Education at Entry | Mean Occupational Prestige | | | | | |
| | First Job | | One Year after Entry | | Two Years after Entry | |
	White	Black	White	Black	White	Black
No high school	22.7	21.4	22.6	21.4	23.1	21.6
Some high school	26.5	23.9	27.3	24.2	29.1	24.5
High school graduate	28.3	26.0	29.8	27.7	31.0	28.5
Some college	32.7	29.9	33.1	31.2	34.5	31.4
College graduate	46.0	38.5	48.6	39.2	48.6	42.1
Total	29.3	24.8	30.5	25.5	31.7	26.0
Missing values (percent)	.7	.3	.5	.7	.2	.7
Total number of cases	850	738	850	738	850	738

men of both races with no high school, or among blacks with some high
school.

Relatively similar patterns appear in wages over the same period[2]
(see Table 3.6). The mean white wage grows by $50 per month, to $293,
but the black mean increases by only $26 per month, to $226. As with the
prestige scores, the wage increase of whites is twice as great as that for
blacks; however these two results are independent, since the correlations
between wages and prestige are not large enough to account for the
similarity. Men with more education make greater wage gains over the 2
years; the increase for men with no high school is $42 per month, for high
school graduates it is $50, and for college graduates, $77. The corresponding values for blacks are $13, $39, and $66 per month. Again there is

[2] The wages of respondents at the point 1 and 2 years after entry is extrapo-
lated from the wage values at the start and at the end of the job, since only these two
wage values are available.

TABLE 3.5 DISTRIBUTION OF OCCUPATIONAL PRESTIGE OF FIRST JOB AFTER ENTRY AND TWO YEARS
AFTER ENTRY, BY EDUCATION AT THE TIME AND RACE

Education, Race, and Job	Occupational Prestige (percent)					Number of cases
	Under 20	20-29.9	30 or more	Armed Forces	Total	
No high school						
White						
First job	62	21	13	4	100	131
Two years after entry	57	19	13	11	100	130
Black						
First job	66	23	10	1	100	184
Two years after entry	64	25	10	1	100	184
Some high school						
White						
First job	32	17	29	24	100	178
Two years after entry	18	19	25	38	100	174
Black						
First job	45	19	14	22	100	258
Two years after entry	40	18	13	29	100	255
High school graduate						
White						
First job	31	22	32	15	100	363
Two years after entry	12	16	31	41	100	367
Black						
First job	30	33	18	19	100	221
Two years after entry	14	23	18	45	100	220

TABLE 3.6   MEAN WAGES AT START OF FIRST JOB AFTER ENTRY AND ONE AND TWO YEARS AFTER ENTRY, BY EDUCATION AT THE TIME AND RACE

| | Wages ($/month) | | | | | |
| | At Start of First Job | | One Year after Entry | | Two Years after Entry | |
Education	White	Black	White	Black	White	Black
No high school	149	142	155	148	191	155
Some high school	230	200	239	213	263	224
High school graduate	249	222	270	244	296	261
Some college	272	281	304	339	346	364
College graduate	354	294	390	321	431	362
Total	243	200	261	214	293	226
Number of cases	618	526	536	482	489	453
In the armed forces (percent)	16.8	16.1	28.3	23.4	34.4	27.8
Missing values (percent)	10.5	12.6	8.9	11.2	8.0	10.8
Total number of cases	850	738	850	738	850	738

evidence of a worsening of the position of men with the lowest amounts of education, a pattern that is more pronounced for blacks.

Though there is a clear tendency for individuals with more education to make greater prestige and wage gains in the 2 years after entry, as the tabulations show, these relationships are not very strong. The correlations between educational attainment and the increase in prestige over the first 2 years are only .037 for whites and .140 for blacks; the corresponding correlations for the increase in wages during this period amount to .155 for whites and .221 for blacks. These values compare to correlations between education and prestige scores of the order of .5, and between education and wages of about .4. So it proves much easier to predict the level of job than the extent of mobility over this period. The correlations between prestige score of first job and increase in prestige are all (i.e., for the first year and the first 2 years after entry, for both races) negative, as are the corresponding wage measures, since it is the men who start out with the poorest jobs who experience the most upward mobility.

Changes in the distributions of occupational prestige and wages can be linked to the patterns of first job durations. It is the men with the least education who have the longest first job durations. Many of them are still on their first jobs at the points 1 and 2 years after entry—which certainly helps to account for the lack of change in prestige, since, by definition, an individual must change jobs in order for his prestige score to rise. Wages, on the other hand, can change during the course of a job, so this constraint does not apply. Approximately equal increases in prestige scores and wages of jobs take place in the first and second years after entry.

The proportion of men in the armed forces grows rapidly in the first year after entry and also increases considerably in the second year (see Table 3.7). Of the white respondents, 17% have first jobs in the armed forces, another 12% join in the first year after entry and a further 6% in the second year after entry. For blacks the increases are not so great; 16% take first jobs in the armed forces, and the proportions increase by 7% and 4% in the first and second years. Men with uncompleted units of education, those with *some* high school and *some* college are more likely to take first jobs in the armed forces than are high school and college graduates; in the 2 years after entry this difference disappears, except that white college graduates are still less likely to enter the service than are whites with some college. Few of the men with the least education enter the armed forces; of those with no high school, only 1.1% of the blacks and 11.5% of the

TABLE 3.7   PERCENT WITH FIRST JOB IN ARMED FORCES AND IN ARMED FORCES ONE AND TWO
              YEARS AFTER ENTRY, BY EDUCATION AT THE TIME AND RACE

| Education at the Time | Percent in the Armed Forces | | | | | |
| | First Job | | One Year after Entry | | Two Years after Entry | |
	White	Black	White	Black	White	Black
No high school	5	1	8	1	12	1
Some high school	24	21	31	25	38	29
High school graduate	15	19	30	35	41	45
Some college	29	31	45	39	43	37
College graduate	16	28	29	44	27	36
Total	16.8	16.1	28.3	23.4	34.4	27.8

whites join the armed forces in the 2 years after entry. These small
proportions are no doubt a function of the low mean age at entry of this
group, but age does not explain the racial difference since the ages of
whites and blacks in this category are very similar.

Clearly, the number of jobs held in the first 2 years after entry must
be related to the durations of those jobs—groups with low durations
should hold more jobs. We obtain some additional information from an
examination of the number of jobs held. In the first year after entry, 64%
of the white respondents and 79% of the blacks do not change jobs, and a
year later 42% of whites and 61% of blacks still have not changed jobs (see
Table 3.8). As was the case for duration of first job, the relationship
between number of jobs held and education is nonlinear. In order of
increasing mobility, the ranking of the five main categories of education is:
no high school, some high school, college graduate, some college, and high
school graduate. The ranking is the same for both races, and the same
results are obtained whether the proportion of men with more than one
job or the average number of jobs held is used as the index of mobility.
Though the pattern is very consistent, educational attainment once more
proves to be a rather poor predictor, explaining only about 5% of the
variance in the number of jobs held.

TABLE 3.8 NUMBER OF JOBS HELD IN THE FIRST YEAR AND FIRST TWO YEARS AFTER ENTRY, BY EDUCATION AT THE TIME AND RACE

Time Period, Race, and Education at Entry	Number of Jobs Held					Mean	Standard Deviation	Number of Cases
	Percentage Distribution							
	1	2	3	4 or more	Total			
First year after entry								
White								
No high school	84	11	3	2	100	1.23	.61	131
Some high school	70	25	4	1	100	1.34	.58	177
High school graduate	56	31	10	3	100	1.61	.81	366
Some college	66	27	5	2	100	1.45	.75	84
College graduate	52	35	11	2	100	1.63	.77	91
Total	64	27	7	2	100	1.75	.75	850
Black								
No high school	91	7	2	0	100	1.10	.35	184
Some high school	85	14	1	0	100	1.16	.38	259
High school graduate	66	28	6	0	100	1.41	.60	221
Some college	69	23	4	4	100	1.38	.67	49
College graduate	68	28	4	0	100	1.36	.56	25
Total	79	18	3	0	100	1.24	.50	738
First two years after entry								
White								
No high school	62	25	10	3	100	1.58	.93	130
Some high school	47	34	13	6	100	1.82	.98	174
High school graduate	35	36	19	10	100	2.09	1.09	369
Some college	40	49	5	6	100	1.77	.84	84
College graduate	41	33	18	8	100	1.96	1.04	92
Total	42	35	15	8	100	1.91	1.04	850
Black								
No high school	77	15	4	3	100	1.34	.71	184
Some high school	64	27	7	2	100	1.48	.74	258
High school graduate	47	39	10	4	100	1.73	.82	222
Some college	55	35	4	6	100	1.56	.76	49
College graduate	64	20	16	0	100	1.52	.77	25
Total	61	28	8	3	100	1.53	.78	738

The relationship between education and the two measures of job quality grows stronger over the first 2 years. For whites, educational attainment explains 32.6% of the variance in prestige scores of the first job and 36.9% of the variance at the point 2 years after entry; the black variance rises from 24.3% to 28.9%. The corresponding wage variances increase from 19.1% to 22.9% for whites and, strikingly, from 12.6% to 21.7% for blacks. So, the first 2 years after entry are marked by some falling into line of education and job quality—presumably men whose first jobs are below what they expect from their education search for better ones, since it is unlikely that those with jobs above what the average person with the same level of education could expect would want to change jobs. We should note that the wage correlations are based only on the respondents with civilian jobs, so men who had low-paying jobs and, as an alternative, enter the armed forces remove themselves from the correlation.

To summarize, the increases in prestige and wage levels in the 2 years after entry are not large. Yet, the way in which they are distributed increases the inequality between blacks and whites and significantly worsens the position of whites and blacks with no high school and of blacks with some high school. The mobility trends and durations of the first job demonstrate similar patterns: whites are more likely than blacks to change jobs; and the lowest level of education (the two lowest levels for blacks) is characterized by markedly longer first job durations. These poorly educated men are also the least likely to enter the armed forces. This comparison of groups is of limited usefulness for the differences found do not explain much of the variation in job duration, wage increases during the first job, or number of jobs held. But they are suggestive. The next chapter will pursue these questions to their conclusion, with an analysis of individual outcomes.

PRESTIGE AND WAGE REGRESSIONS
2 YEARS AFTER ENTRY

Let us now repeat the regression analysis carried out in the previous chapter for first job after entry, this time using prestige scores and wages 2 years after entry as the dependent variables. This makes it possible to

TABLE 3.9 REGRESSION OF OCCUPATIONAL PRESTIGE TWO YEARS AFTER ENTRY ON
FAMILY BACKGROUND, EDUCATION TWO YEARS AFTER ENTRY, NUMBER OF
JOBS BEFORE ENTRY, AND CHARACTERISTICS OF THE JOB HELD, BY RACE

Independent Variable	Regression Coefficient		Standardized Regression Coefficient		Correlation with Dependent Variable	
	White	Black	White	Black	White	Black
Family background						
Father's education	-.05	.62	-.009	.111	.268	.315
Mother's education	.50	-.25	.072*	-.042	.286	.254
Father's occupation	.023	.074	.025	.098*	.262	.259
Number of siblings	.04	-.04	.010	-.018	-.180	-.148
Education two years after entry						
Some high school	4.9	.4	.170*	.019	-.116	-.076
High school graduate	6.1	3.2	.261*	.163*	-.049	.091
Some college	9.6	5.8	.249*	.162*	.084	.152
College graduate	17.0	15.8	.458*	.320*	.517	.288
Number of jobs before entry						
Full-time	-.27	-.07	-.050	-.001	.325	.113
Part-time	.52	-.07	.082*	-.053	.314	.074
Job held two years after entry						
Marital status	.8	-2.0	.028	-.044	.283	.025
Method of locating job						
Direct	2.7	2.1	.115*	.114*	.215	.191
Promotion	5.6	1.9	.128*	.027	.195	.020
Industry						
Military service	1.2	5.9	.051	.294*	-.098	.283
Manufacturing	4.0	1.8	.133*	.079	.079	-.065
Transportation	5.4	1.9	.107*	.034	.081	-.028
Trade	-.1	.9	-.003	.034	-.085	-.117
Finance & public admin.	8.5	1.9	.120	.036	.206	.166
Service	13.1	4.7	.286*	.156*	.392	.175
Regression constant	18.4*	18.3*				

* Statistically significant at .01

discover changes in the relationship between the quality of the job held 2 years after entry, and family background, education, and jobs held before entry, as well as a fourth group of variables—marital status, method of locating the job, and industry of the job held two years after entry. To some extent these changes are limited by the fact that about 40% of white respondents and 60% of black respondents are still in their first jobs at the point 2 years after entry. The regressions differ from those carried out for the first job in that two of the variables—those measuring moves between entry and starting the first job, and the distance of those moves—are no longer used. The prestige regression is in Table 3.9, the wage regression Table 3.11, and Table 3.10 contains a breakdown of the explained variances. (The corresponding results for the first job are in Tables 2.17, 2.18, and 2.19.)

The nineteen independent variables together explain 46.5% of the variance in whites prestige scores, 32.4% for blacks (see Table 3.9). These variances are larger than those obtained for the first job, which amounted to 38.8% and 28.7% respectively. So, the occupational achievement process becomes more predictable in this interval. The most important direct influences on the prestige score of the job held 2 years after entry are the respondent's education, the industry of the job, and the method by which the job is located. Family background and pre-entry job experiences have little direct effect. For whites, mother's education and the number of part-time jobs both have small but statistically significant effects; for blacks, father's prestige score and father's education both have small positive effects on prestige of job. There is an important racial difference in the four regression coefficients for education. Though the ranges of the sets of education variables, 17.0 points for whites and 15.8 points for blacks, are quite similar, the relative positions of the three middle categories differ. Whites with some high school have jobs averaging 4.9 points above the lowest group, those with no high school, but the corresponding difference for blacks is only 0.4 points; white high school graduates have jobs ranking 6.1 points above the lowest group, for blacks the comparable difference is 3.2 points.

Again, jobs found by "direct" methods average 2 to 3 points above those located through family and friends. Jobs obtained through promotion still are better for whites, but not for blacks. The industry of the job again has considerable influence on prestige scores, though its impact is much greater for whites. Jobs in the primary industries and construction,

TABLE 3.10 PROPORTION OF VARIANCE EXPLAINED IN REGRESSION ANALYSES OF OCCUPATIONAL PRESTIGE AND WAGES TWO YEARS AFTER ENTRY, BY FOUR GROUPS OF VARIABLES, BY RACE

	Percent of Variance Explained							
	White				Black			
Dependent Variable and Group of Independent Variables	Zero-Order	Unique	Addi-tional	Cumu-lative	Zero-Order	Unique	Addi-tional	Cumu-lative
Occupational prestige two years after entry								
Family background	11.6	0.5	11.6	11.6	11.3	2.3	11.3	11.3
Education two years after entry	34.0	8.8	23.0	34.6	22.7	9.3	15.3	26.6
Number of jobs before entry	14.8	0.6	1.2	35.8	1.5	0.3	0.1	27.7
Job held two years after entry	33.8	10.7	10.7	46.5	18.4	5.7	5.7	32.4
Wages two years after entry								
Family background	7.1	1.4	7.1	7.1	6.5	1.2	6.5	6.5
Education two years after entry	17.6	1.1	7.3	14.4	17.6	7.1	12.2	18.7
Number of jobs before entry	14.0	3.1	3.5	17.9	1.2	0.1	0.1	18.8
Job held two years after entry	9.7	3.0	3.0	20.9	10.0	2.9	2.9	21.7

and in wholesale and retail trade rank lowest, the ones in manufacturing, transportation, and finance and public administration are in the middle, and the service industry (which includes many professional jobs) ranks highest. The magnitudes of the coefficients are considerably smaller for blacks, and there are also some differences in the ranking of the six industrial categories. Perhaps the most interesting of the racial differences, however, is in the relative standing of jobs in the armed forces, which have coefficients of 1.2 for whites, and 5.9 for blacks. This places military jobs near the bottom of the civilian industries for whites, and at the very top for blacks. So, holding background and education of the respondent constant, the prospect of entering the forces is likely to be more attractive to blacks. A comparison of the explained variances, in Table 3.10, for this regression and those obtained for the first job after entry shows them to be very similar.

The wage regression was again performed on the subset of respondents in civilian jobs after 2 years in the labor force. Since many of the men who change jobs enter the armed forces, this regression contains a larger proportion of individuals who are still in their first jobs than does the prestige regression. All of the variables explain 20.9% of the variation in wages 2 years after entry for whties, 21.7% for blacks—their similarity represents a considerable contrast to the values obtained when wage at the start of the first job was the dependent variables (in Table 2.18); then, the corresponding variances were 28.1% for whites and 15.3% for blacks. A comparison of Table 2.19 and Table 3.10 shows that, for whites, the effect of family background declines from 11.5% to 7.1%; it increases from 3.8% to 6.5% for blacks, and that this accounts for most of the convergence of the totals. Again, family background exerts little direct effect on wages, though mother's education has a significant positive effect for both races; and father's education has a negative effect for whites. Education again exerts a much stronger effect on black wages than on white wages. The range of the black education coefficients is $162 per month, compared to $100 for whites. Since whites earn more than blacks with equal education, more of the impact of their education is mediated by other variables, particularly by pre-entry jobs and the variables describing the job held. Whites gain $12 per month for each full-time job and $13.5 for each part-time job held before entry, but such jobs have little impact on black wages.

Married men have jobs averaging about $30 per month more than single men, and those found by direct methods are about $30 per month

TABLE 3.11   REGRESSION OF WAGES TWO YEARS AFTER ENTRY ON FAMILY BACKGROUND,
EDUCATION TWO YEARS AFTER ENTRY, NUMBER OF JOBS BEFORE ENTRY,
AND CHARACTERISTICS OF THE JOB HELD, BY RACE

Independent Variable	Regression Coefficient		Standardized Regression Coefficient		Correlation with Dependent Variable	
	White	Black	White	Black	White	Black
Family background						
Father's education	-11.1	-3.2	-.116*	-.036	.128	.181
Mother's education	11.5	12.8	.102†	.137†	.212	.245
Father's occupation	.66	-.29	.044	-.025	.165	.103
Number of siblings	-4.0	-1.0	-.067	-.029	-.201	-.114
Education two years after entry						
Some high school	31	46	.066	.159*	-.077	-.012
High school graduate	34	76	.089	.233*	.013	.148
Some college	73	162	.109†	.275*	.091	.257
College graduate	99	161	.171†	.199*	.284	.183
Number of jobs before entry						
Full-time	11.8	-4.3	.133*	-.031	.336	.089
Part-time	13.5	.3	.138*	.002	.297	.090
Job held two years after entry						
Marital status	29	31	.063	.083†	.234	.186
Method of locating job						
Direct	33	30	.085†	.108*	.126	.189
Promotion	54	34	.077	.032	.132	.021
Industry						
Manufacturing	7	14	.016	.044	.065	.084
Transportation	15	0	.023	.000	.043	.015
Trade	-55	-16	-.110*	-.047	-.096	-.058
Finance & public admin.	-43	42	-.045	.060	.043	.164
Service	-32	-8	-.052	-.019	.099	.067
Regression constant	200	153				

* Statistically significant at .01
† Statistically significant at .05

better than those located by family and friends. Men who are promoted into the jobs held 2 years after entry also have higher wages, by $54 for whites and $34 for blacks, compared to jobs found through family and friends. The industry of this job has almost no impact on its wage rate. An examination of the explained variances shows that the chief racial difference lies in the weaker effect of education and the greater impact of pre-entry jobs on white wages.

There is a strong similarity between the regressions examined here and those obtained for the first job after entry. The differences which are found amount more to change in the relative importance of particular variables, rather than to a shift in the basic relationships. The most important change is in the explained variances for the wage variable—the starting wages of the first job is almost twice as predictable for whites as it is for blacks, but 2 years after entry the racial difference is close to zero.

PATH ANALYSIS OF THE FIRST 2 YEARS AFTER ENTRY

Because the men with jobs in the armed forces do not earn wages comparable to those of civilians, the relationship between military service and wages cannot be properly defined. So we have produced two pairs (one for blacks and one for whites) of path diagrams, one of which includes three variables measuring whether the respondent's first job and his jobs 1 and 2 years after entry are in the military or in the civilian labor force, but no wage values. The second pair of path diagrams includes both wages and prestige scores, but no military service variable. In this latter case the relationships between wages and all the other variables are computed on a "pairwise present" basis that excludes cases in which either variable is missing—so the relationship between the wages of men in the armed forces and all other variables is assumed to be the same as for civilian jobs. This analysis differs from that presented in Chapter 2 in that it does not include age at entry. The discussion is restricted to the period after entry. Because the temporal ordering of the variables is well defined, the selection of paths presents no difficulties.[3]

---

[3] As our examination of the period of unemployment before entry shows, a number of individuals, mostly in the lower categories of education, had not found

We take first the analysis in Figure 3.1, which includes prestige scores and military service. The only direct effect on whites' first jobs is education at entry—the path coefficient is .519. For blacks, the direct effect of education on first job prestige score is only about one-half as great, and there are sizable direct effects on this prestige variable from father's education, father's occupation, and the variable indicating whether or not the first job was in the armed forces—all of them positive. For both races, there is a positive path from respondent's education to the military service variable, showing that men with more education are more likely to serve, though the effect is about three times stronger for blacks than whites.

The largest effect on the prestige score of the job held 1 year after entry is from the prestige score of the first job, which reflects the fact that many of the respondents had the same job at both points. This effect of the first job is much stronger for blacks, since they experience less mobility. Education at entry also directly affects this prestige value. Military service has a positive direct effect for blacks only. Naturally, the variable measuring whether or not the first job is in the armed forces is the strongest predictor of military service at the point 1 year after entry; but what is revealing is the fact that military service has a *positive* path from education for blacks and a *negative* path from prestige score of first job for whites. So, whites with poorer first jobs are more likely to join the armed forces than whites with better jobs. No such effect appears for blacks.

For both whites and blacks, the prestige score 2 years after entry has positive paths from the first job, the job held a year after entry, and education; there is a negative path from military service 2 years after entry for whites, a positive one for blacks. Again the effect of previous jobs is stronger, and that of education weaker, for blacks. There are small effects from part-time and full-time jobs and from the number of siblings. The path analysis shows the greater mobility of whites, the fact that occupa-

---

their first jobs by the point 1 year after entry. These proportions amount to 6% of the white sample, 9% of the black sample. For this small group the point one year after entry precedes the first job variables. The substitution procedure employed, which takes the nearest job when the respondent does not hold one at the point exactly after entry, results in the first job and the one held a year after entry being defined as the same job, and this will be one that occurs more than 1 year after entry. So the temporal ordering is not affected. The number of such cases is small and has little effect on the path analysis.

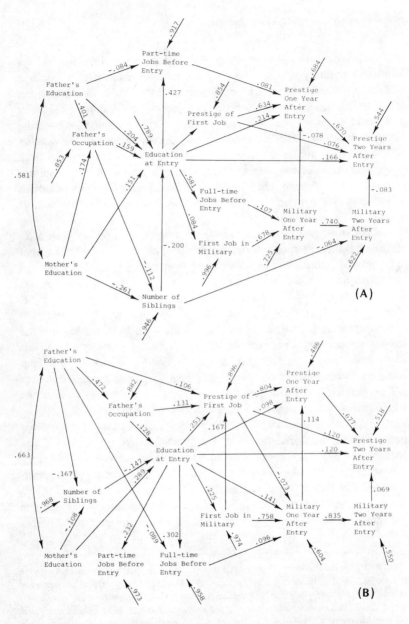

Figure 3.1. Path model to the point two years after entry, with prestige and military service, (a) whites and (b) blacks.

tional mobility is dependent on education, and the contrasting effects of military service on black and white prestige scores.

The second set of path diagrams, in Figure 3.2, incorporates three prestige and three wage variables. Educational attainment has direct effects on all six of these variables for both races. The paths between education and the prestige variables have greater magnitudes for whites, while those connecting education to wages are stronger for blacks—a pattern also observed in the large regressions. The lower rates of mobility for blacks, which give rise to stronger paths among the prestige variables in the first path analysis, are found for both the prestige and the wage variables in these diagrams. This pattern is more marked for wages than for prestige because the men who leave their first jobs and go into the armed forces disappear from the corresponding wage correlations. The path coefficient from the wage 1 year after entry to that 2 years after entry has a value of .999, which is counteracted by a negative path, with the value −.176, from the starting wage of the first job.

Because the choice of a job seems to be dictated, for the large part of the population that does not have very specific occupational skills, as much by wage as by prestige considerations, the connection between prestige and wage variables defined at the same point in time is shown by calculating the correlations between their residuals. Three such values, for the first job and the jobs at points 1 and 2 years after entry are shown. None of them is as large as .2. In each case the white correlations are larger. For example, for the first job the correlations between the residuals amount to .148 for whites and .113 for blacks.[4]

---

[4] If direct effects are allowed from the prestige score of a job to the wage of that job, the modifications in the path diagram are as follows:

Path to	From	White	Black
Wages of the first job	Mother's education	.138	—
	Number of siblings	−.070	—
	Education at entry	.131	.315
	Full-time jobs before entry	.115	—
	Part-time jobs before entry	.113	—
	Prestige of the first job	.142	.113
	Residual	.883	.931

It is possible for prestige variables to affect wage values at later points in time, and vice versa. Only one such path is found, whites' wages 1 year after entry have a small direct effect on prestige score 2 years after entry. The path diagrams make it clear that the dynamics of the prestige and wage dimensions of job quality operate quite separately in the first 2 years after entry. The lower correlations between the residuals of blacks show that the relationship is weaker for blacks than for whites.

There are a number of small direct effects from pre-entry jobs and from family background, but they are of little importance. The only visible pattern is found in the positive paths from number of full-time and number of part-time jobs before entry to white wages at the start of the first job and 1 year after entry. The effects of family background on jobs are almost entirely indirect, and they are routed through the respondents' education.

SUMMARY

There is not a great deal of mobility in the 2 years after entry, but what mobility does take place is disproportionately distributed among the

Path to	From	White	Black
Wages 1 year after entry	Father's education	—	−.057
	Mother's education	—	.069
	Full-time jobs before entry	.070	—
	Part-time jobs before entry	.052	.046
	Wages of the first job	.765	.892
	Prestige 1 year after entry	.089	.064
	Residual	.538	.401
Wages 2 years after entry	Father's education	−.066	—
	Mother's education	—	.063
	Full-time jobs before entry	.069	—
	Wages of the first job	.342	−.178
	Prestige 1 year after entry	−.119	—
	Wages 1 year after entry	.421	1.030
	Prestige 2 years after entry	.177	—
	Residual	.634	.463

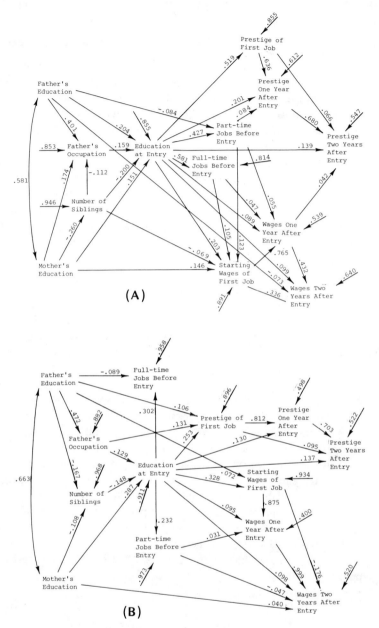

Figure 3.2. Path model to the point two years after entry, with prestige and wages. (a) Whites. Correlations of residuals: full-time and part-time jobs before entry = .342, Prestige and wages: first job after entry = .113, one year after entry = .120, two years after entry = .048. (b) Blacks. Correlations of residuals: full-time and part-time jobs before entry = .219, Prestige and wages: first job after entry = .147, one year after entry = .227, two years after entry = .124.

levels of education and between blacks and whites, increasing the differences found in the analysis of the first job after entry. So, the question as to which respondents experience greater mobility can be very easily answered—men with more education and whites. Three measures of the rewards that could be obtained during the first job—wage increases, on-the-job training, and promotions—were distributed in the same way. However, it is significant that the relationships between wage increase and the three variables educational attainment, wage at the *start* of the job, and its prestige score are very weak—so the conventional indicators of the level of this job are not very accurate predictors of changes during the job.

In the first 2 years after entry, 6 out of 10 white respondents and 4 out of 10 black respondents change jobs. The lowest rates of job mobility and the greatest first job durations are found among blacks and whites with no high school and among blacks with some high school. It is these three groups that experience the smallest prestige and wage increases. The average first job lasts about 2 years for whites and 3 years for blacks, both these values being disproportionately increased by small numbers of very long first jobs. Just as education is a poor predictor of wage and prestige mobility in the 2 years after entry, it has quite weak effects on the number of jobs held and on the duration of the first job. In general, our models are much less successful in dealing with mobility processes than in predicting the levels of the first job or of the jobs held 1 and 2 years after entry. The mobility *within* racial and educational categories is far more important than the differences between those categories.

When the large regression analyses of the prestige score of the first job after entry and the starting wage of that job are repeated, using the values of these variables at the point 2 years after entry, there is little change in the prestige results, though the explained variances do increase. The most interesting change is in the explained variances of the wage regressions—the starting wage of the first job is much less predictable for blacks than for whites, but in the 2 years after entry this difference disappears.

Social Mobility after Entry

The phenomenon we know in the aggregate as social mobility, whether it takes place between one generation and the next or within a generation, is in fact a sum of many smaller changes between jobs, locations, kinds of hosueholds, and so on. The study of these individual steps in the larger process can do much to provide an understanding of the nature of the decisions that create the patterns we observe. Particularly crucial for the study of occupational mobility are those changes that occur in the first years of labor force experience. Using artificially constructed 10-year cohorts, Blau and Duncan (1967:184) show that job mobility declines as men get older; Zeller *et al.* (1970:29) and Saben (1967) find that decreases in job mobility are clearly visible by the age of 21. This chapter investigates job changes in the period just after entry into the labor force, focusing on individual differences in mobility and the rewards of changing jobs, rather than on the impact of mobility on individuals of each race and in broad educational categories.

The analysis deals with three fundamental questions:

1. *Is it possible to classify individual respondents according to their rates of job mobility?* While there is a great deal of variation in the duration of the first job, we do not know whether some individuals can be characterized, over some longer period, as having consistently higher or lower levels of mobility. Thus men with shorter first jobs need not have second jobs that are also of shorter than average duration.

2. *Why do men change jobs?* This is an extension of the previous question. Two different kinds of factors that influence an individual's decision to change jobs can be distinguished: his own characteristics—his

103

level of education, previous work experience, race, age, temperament, and so on; and second, characteristics of the situation in which he finds himself—such as the rate of pay and working conditions of the job he already holds, whether or not he has found another, better job, and his desire to find some other kind of work. The two factors are not completely separable; for example, whites have better jobs than blacks. Nor is either one fully measured in this study. But the analytic distinction is a useful one, and it is central to the argument presented here. The methodological implication of this way of thinking about the problem is that multivariate analysis must somehow be applied to the mobility observed, so as to distinguish these competing individual and situational factors.

3. *Does it pay to change jobs?* It is one thing to analyze the factors that affect each step from one job to another, quite another to decide whether the individuals who change jobs are better off as a result. Though an individual can experience wage mobility without changing jobs, mobility in the prestige dimension (or within any *occupational* ranking scheme) necessarily involves changing jobs in order to change occupations.[1] But do high rates of mobility in the first years of labor force experience necessarily confer benefits on the "movers"—especially if a comparison is made between more and less mobile individuals with the same levels of education and of other resources?

Before proceeding to the analysis, it is useful to review the results obtained in the previous chapter, though they only apply to the groups of respondents in the five main educational categories. It was found that the categories of respondents with the largest increases in mean occupational prestige scores and wages in the 2 years after entry were the ones with the lowest first job durations and the highest numbers of jobs in the first 2 years after entry. Blacks have consistently lower rates of movement between jobs, and they experience considerably less prestige and wage mobility in this period. The results are certainly suggestive. It appears that changing jobs does result in greater prestige and wage mobility, and the

---

[1] Remember, the definition of *job* used in this analysis means that a respondent changes jobs when he changes employers or when he changes occupations though continuing to work for the same firm. However, the fact that only 11.7% of the white respondents and 5.8% of the blacks gained their second jobs by promotion, whereas the remainder changed firms, shows that the impact of movement within firms is limited.

fact that the higher rates are associated with two other beneficial characteristics, more education and being white, strengthens the case. However,
it should be recognized that the differences observed are relatively small,
explaining of the order of 5% of the variance in first job durations and in
number of jobs held. Though extremely consistent, these patterns are far
weaker than those obtained in the analysis of prestige scores and wages of
these jobs. This chapter completes the analysis of job changes begun above
by examining individual experiences in the period just after entry into the
labor force.

IS JOB DURATION AN "INDIVIDUAL" VARIABLE?

The most obvious test of the existence of personal "styles" of job
holding simply involves examining the relationship among durations of
jobs held by each individual. For whites, the correlation between the first
and second job durations is 0.171, for blacks it is 0.139.[2] These values
show that there is some association (significant at .001) between the
lengths of the first and second jobs, and their magnitudes are considerably
larger than could be accounted for by the relationships between job
duration and respondents' education. Yet the explained variance, amounting to less than 3% for each race, certainly suggests that other factors have
a great deal more influence on job mobility. The same conclusion emerges
from an analysis of job changes in the first 2 years after entry. Among the
men who hold only one job in the first year, 33.4% of the whites and
22.3% of the blacks change jobs in their second year. By comparison, of
the men who hold two or more jobs in their first year, 35.5% of the whites
and 28.6% of the blacks make another job change in the next year. The
differences have the predicted direction but are so weak that we must
conclude that the length of time spent on a job is only marginally related
to the characteristics of the individual.

[2] The men who hold only one job between entry and the time of the interview
are excluded from this correlation, since the duration of their second jobs is
undefined. For the men who hold more than two jobs, it is found that the
correlations among the durations of the first and second jobs and those of later jobs
are positive and of the same order as the correlation between the durations of the
first two jobs.

PREDICTING THE NUMBER OF JOBS HELD

An analysis of variance revealed that education explains only 3.6% of the variation in the number of jobs whites hold in the first 2 years after they enter the labor force; and the proportion is just a bit larger, 4.3% for blacks. In order to determine what other characteristic of the individual or his situation might do more to explain mobility in this period, the number of jobs held in the first 2 years after entry was subjected to a regression analysis like that carried out for the prestige and wage variables. Men who were in the armed forces during the interval were obliged to serve for at least 2 years, and because of this obvious constraint on their mobility they are excluded from the regression.

The measures used to predict the number of jobs held include the four family background variables, number of full-time and part-time jobs before entry, respondent's education, his marital status, prestige score and wages of the job held 2 years after entry, how that job was located, and the industry of the job. The twenty variables explain 13.9% of the variation in the number of jobs held by whites; for blacks, they explain 9.2% of the variation.[3] So, neither this elaboration of the characteristics of the individual nor the more detailed description of the job held by him 2 years after entry enables us to explain more than a small proportion of the variance in mobility during this 2-year period. The regression is in Table 4.1.

Few of the regression coefficients are large enough to be statistically significant, although this in itself is an interesting finding. The four family background variables exert small and contradictory effects on the number of jobs held. For example, whites whose mothers have more education hold more jobs, as do those with *more* siblings. Although a much larger sample might allow us to make some sense out of these results, they have very much the appearance of random error. The predominant (but again statistically insignificant) effect of pre-entry work experience is to increase job mobility after entry by a small amount, the negative regression

---

[3] Most of the respondents hold between one and three jobs in the 2 years after entry. The regression is quite similar to a discriminant function analysis with the number of jobs held classified into only two categories: one job, and two or more jobs. A "pairwise present" correlation matrix, which substitutes for missing cases by using the relationships between each pair of variables for those cases where both variables' values are known, was used in this regression.

TABLE 4.1   REGRESSION OF NUMBER OF JOBS HELD IN THE FIRST TWO
YEARS AFTER ENTRY ON FAMILY BACKGROUND, EDUCATION
AT ENTRY, NUMBER OF JOBS BEFORE ENTRY, AND
CHARACTERISTICS OF THE JOB HELD TWO YEARS AFTER
ENTRY, BY RACE, FOR MEN IN CIVILIAN JOBS AT THE
POINT TWO YEARS AFTER ENTRY

Independent Variable	Regression Coefficient		Standardized Regression Coefficient	
	White	Black	White	Black
Family background				
Father's education	-.01	-.03	-.025	-.005
Mother's education	.06	-.04	.091	-.067
Father's occupation	-.003	-.008	-.039	-.013
Number of siblings	.03	-.01	.077	-.034
Education two years after entry				
Some high school	.38	.11	.138*	.069
High school graduate	.44	.33	.201*	.178*
Some college	.18	.40	.048	.120†
College graduate	.13	.34	.038	.073
Number of jobs before entry				
Full-time	.04	-.03	.084	-.035
Part-time	.05	.07	.082	.089
Job held two years after entry				
Marital status	.17	.02	.062	.010
Method of locating job				
Direct	.30	.22	.139*	.139*
Promotion	.69	.58	.170*	.095†
Industry				
Manufacturing	-.03	-.01	-.011	-.007
Transportation	-.04	.03	-.010	.006
Trade	-.23	.11	-.082	.054
Finance and public administration	.32	.21	.059	.052
Service	-.19	.11	-.054	.049
Occupational prestige	-.011	-.010	-.140†	-.122†
Wages	.0083	.0012	.145*	.121
Regression constant	.04	.05		
Percent of variance explained by all variables	13.8	9.2		

†   Statistically significant at .05
*   Statistically significant at .01

coefficient for number of full-time jobs for blacks is overcome by the larger positive coefficient for number of part-time jobs. This makes sense; more work experience appears to lead to increased mobility.

Educational attainment at entry has a statistically significant impact on the number of jobs held, though the ordering of the five categories of education is somewhat different from that obtained at the zero-order level (in Table 3.1). For whites, the highest rates of mobility are found among the men with some high school and high school graduates, followed by the groups with some college and college graduates; the least mobile group is that of the men with no high school. In the black sample, the three top groups, high school graduates and above, have the most jobs, the men with some high school are in the middle, and the group with no high school is again lowest. Three important conclusions are suggested: The relationship between education and the number of jobs held is curvilinear, it is not the same for blacks and whites, and men with the least education—those with no high school—have the lowest rates of mobility.

Married white respondents appear to hold a slightly larger number of jobs than unmarried whites, although the difference is not large enough to be statistically significant; for blacks, the difference is virtually zero. The way in which the job held at the point 2 years after entry was located is significantly related to the number of jobs held. Men who use "direct" methods to locate the job they hold 2 years after entry, have more jobs than those who rely on their families and friends to find this job. It makes sense to find that these more gregarious individuals change jobs more often; the controls on family background and education mean that this result is not simply a class difference. The second finding, that men who are promoted into the jobs they hold 2 years after entry have held more jobs, is tautological—to have been promoted they must have held at least one other job in the period after entry (except for the very few respondents whose work for an employer began before entry). None of the five dummy industry variables for either race is statistically significant; though again a large sample might make something of the patterns, it is quite certain that the industry differences cannot be large—at least when it is measured at this crude level.

The last two variables, measuring the prestige score and wage of the job held 2 years after entry, are significantly related to the number of jobs held, though their impact is stronger for whites. Men with *lower* prestige scores and *higher* wages hold more jobs, though the wage effect for blacks is very small. This suggests that increased mobility may result in a trade-off of prestige for wages, which is perhaps the result of a conscious search for higher wages on the part of respondents. The effects of prestige and wages are of sufficient magnitude, at least for whites, to suggest that this trade-off does take place. For blacks, however, the decrease in prestige value is barely compensated by a wage increase, suggesting that blacks fail to make the wage gains they desire. This pattern is relatively weak, and however intriguing the result may be, it accounts for no more than 3% of the variation in the numbers of jobs for whites, and much less for blacks.

The result of this regression is to provide some understanding of the factors associated with changing jobs. But the large number of variables used explains only a small proportion of the differences in mobility. Neither education, family background, extent of early work experience, or the nature of the job held bear much of a relationship to the number of jobs held. Let us now examine more closely the relationship between job changing and occupational achievement.

THE EFFECT OF CHANGING JOBS

Simple economic logic suggests that men with better first jobs will remain at these jobs for longer periods. Zeller *et al.* (1970:35) find that respondents who change jobs during a 1-year period leave jobs whose median rates of pay are *lower* by $.20 per hour for whites and $.25 per hour for blacks than those of the men who do not change jobs. As shown in Table 4.2, we find just the opposite. Whites who change jobs in the first year after entry have first jobs averaging $18 per month *more* than those who remain at the first job for 1 year or more; for blacks the difference amounts to $8 per month. Similar differences ($8 for whites, $15 for blacks) appear in a comparison of the men who change jobs in the first 2 years after entry to those who do not. The wage rates do not vary systematically among the men who hold two, three, or more jobs during this period.

An examination of the prestige scores partially resolves the difference with Zeller *et al.* Men who hold only one job in the first year have *higher* first job prestige scores, by 1.0 points for whites, and by 2.2 points for blacks, than those who change jobs. So the men who do not change

TABLE 4.2   MEAN OCCUPATIONAL PRESTIGE AND STARTING WAGES OF FIRST
            JOB AFTER ENTRY, BY NUMBER OF JOBS HELD IN THE FIRST
            YEAR AND IN THE FIRST TWO YEARS AFTER ENTRY, BY RACE

	Mean Occupational Prestige of the First Job		Mean Starting Wages of the First Job ($/month)	
Number of Jobs Held	White	Black	White	Black
Jobs in the first year after entry				
One	29.7	25.2	235	197
Two or more	28.7	23.0	252	206
Two	29.1	23.1	251	210
Three	27.0	22.6	265	183
Four or more	29.2	17.3†	220	244†
Total	29.3	24.7	243	199
Percent of variance explained by number Of jobs	.3	1.1*	.6	.3
Jobs in the first two years after entry				
One	30.8	25.9	239	193
Two or more	28.3	22.9	247	208
Two	28.9	23.1	243	206
Three	28.1	22.0	256	202
Four	26.6	22.1	252	224
Five or more	25.5	29.6†	244	167†
Total	29.3	24.7	243	199
Percent of variance explained by number of jobs	1.3*	3.1*	.1	.4

*   Statistically significant at .05
†   Less than ten cases

jobs apparently trade prestige for wages. The differences are larger, 2.5 points for whites, and 3.0 points for blacks, if the comparison is made at the point 2 years after entry. In an analysis of variance, the number of jobs held in the first year or in the first 2 years after entry accounts for no more than 3.1% of the variation in first job wages or prestige scores, for blacks or whites. Seven of the eight explained variances in Table 4.2 amount to 1.3% or less. To take one example, the number of jobs held in the first year after entry explains only .3% of the variance in prestige score of the first job for whites—this is no larger a value than could be expected to result from random error.

Still, it is rather disturbing to find that the men who remain longer at their first jobs earn lower wages. This result appears to be an artifact of an oversimplified definition of the problem. A particular job may be a "good" job for one man while it is far below the expectations of another, depending on the education and skills of the individual. A college graduate employed as a technician might be tempted to move to a better position as soon as the opportunity presents itself; a person with only 5 years of elementary school in the same job would be unlikely to do so, for he is much less likely to find a better alternative. It is therefore necessary to compare individuals within categories of educational attainment in order to make sense out of job changes. Such an analysis of the wages of the first job is shown in Table 4.3.

The wages at the start of the first job is regressed on two sets of variables measuring the educational attainment of the respondent and the number of jobs held in the first year after entry. Four dummy variables are again used to measure education, and three dummy variables distinguish individuals who held two, three, and four or more jobs from the group that held only one job in the first year after entry into the labor force. The regression shows that, *with education held constant*, men with more than one job in the first year after entry did indeed have *lower* wages at the start of the first job than men who did not change jobs, though the differences, which average only $3 per month for whites and $17 per month for blacks are not very large. Although it is comforting to find that the men who change jobs have lower paying first jobs, the difference in wages between the "movers" and "stayers" is close to zero. To all practical purposes we can say that wages bear no relationship to the decision to change jobs, once the respondent's education is held constant.

There are, however, meaningful differences in the prestige scores of the first jobs of the "movers" and "stayers"; holding educational attainment constant strengthens the relationships observed at the zero-order level (see Table 4.4). Comparing individuals with equal education, black respondents who hold two jobs in the first year after entry have first jobs with prestige scores averaging 3.9 points below those of men who do not change jobs. The corresponding white difference is 2.4 prestige points. So, the average black respondent who changes jobs was in a relatively worse position, (compared to blacks of equal education who remained in their

TABLE 4.3   REGRESSION OF STARTING WAGE OF FIRST JOB AFTER ENTRY ON NUMBER OF JOBS HELD IN
THE FIRST YEAR AFTER ENTRY AND EDUCATION ONE YEAR AFTER ENTRY, AND ON NUMBER
OF JOBS HELD IN THE FIRST TWO YEARS AFTER ENTRY AND EDUCATION TWO YEARS AFTER
ENTRY, BY RACE

Independent Variable or Group of Variables	Education and Number of Jobs Held after One Year		Education and Number of Jobs Held after Two Years	
	White	Black	White	Black
REGRESSION COEFFICIENTS (IN $/MONTH)				
Education**				
Some high school	84*	59*	85*	61*
High school graduate	104*	85*	108*	81*
Some college	125*	137*	127*	132*
College graduate	207*	157*	208*	155*
Number of jobs held**				
Two	-3	-12	-11	-6
Three	7	-44	-9	-14
Four or more	-39	-34		
Four			-17	22
Five or more			- 4	-48
Regression constant	146*	144*	150*	143*
PERCENT OF VARIANCE EXPLAINED IN STARTING WAGE OF FIRST JOB				
Zero-order effect				
Education	15.7*	11.4*	15.9*	11.0*
Number of jobs	.6	.3	.1	.4
Unique effect				
Education	15.3*	11.7*	16.0*	10.9*
Number of jobs	.2	.6	.2	.3
Total without interaction	16.0*	11.7	16.0*	11.4*
Interaction effect	1.4	1.0	2.2	3.1
Total with interaction	17.4*	12.7*	18.2*	14.5*

* Statistically significant at .05
** The four dummy variables for education measure the impact of the levels of education
relative to the group with no high school. The effect of the number of jobs is relative to the group with only one job.

first jobs) than his white counterpart. So, blacks are less mobile than whites, since it takes a greater prestige difference to make them change jobs. This ties in with the earlier finding, in Table 3.2, that blacks are much less likely to change jobs than are whites.

Four out of five blacks do not change jobs in the first year after entry, compared to about six out of ten whites, yet number of jobs explains more of the variance in the first job prestige scores of blacks than it does of whites; the explained variances are 3.4% for blacks and 1.5% for whites. The corresponding effects for the point 2 years after entry are 5.3%

TABLE 4.4 REGRESSION OF OCCUPATIONAL PRESTIGE OF THE FIRST JOB AFTER ENTRY ON NUMBER OF JOBS HELD IN THE FIRST YEAR AFTER ENTRY AND EDUCATION ONE YEAR AFTER ENTRY, AND ON NUMBER OF JOBS HELD IN THE FIRST TWO YEARS AFTER ENTRY AND EDUCATION TWO YEARS AFTER ENTRY, BY RACE.

Independent Variable or Group of Variables	Education and Number of Jobs Held after One Year		Education and Number of Jobs Held after Two Years	
	White	Black	White	Black
REGRESSION COEFFICIENTS (PRESTIGE POINTS)				
Education**				
Some high school	4.1*	2.7*	4.4*	3.0*
High school graduate	6.4*	5.6*	6.7*	5.8*
Some college	10.4*	9.2*	9.9*	8.9*
College graduate	24.3*	18.0*	24.4*	17.8*
Number of jobs held**				
Two	-2.4*	-3.9*	-2.7*	-3.9*
Three	-5.0*	-4.6*	-3.9*	-5.4*
Four or more	-2.1	-13.6		
Four			-5.9*	-4.0*
Five or more			-5.2	-2.8
Regression constant	23.2*	21.7*	23.9*	22.3*
PERCENT OF VARIANCE EXPLAINED IN STARTING WAGE OF FIRST JOB				
Zero-order effect				
Education	27.7*	14.6*	28.3*	14.5*
Number of jobs	.3	1.1*	1.3*	3.1*
Unique effect				
Education	28.9*	16.8*	29.3*	16.6*
Number of jobs	1.5*	3.4*	2.3*	5.3*
Total without interaction	29.2*	17.9*	30.6*	19.8*
Interaction effect	1.2	1.9	2.0	3.0
Total with interaction	30.4*	19.8*	32.6*	22.7*

* Statistically significant at .05
** The four dummy variables for education measure the impact of the levels of education relative to the group with no high school. The effect of the number of jobs is relative to the group with only one job.

for blacks and 2.3% for whites. So, the group of men who change jobs are more clearly defined as a low prestige group in the black sample than in the white sample. In each case, educational attainment acts as a suppressor variable, the relationship between number of jobs held and prestige score of first job is stronger when education is held constant than at the zero-order level.

The most interesting finding to emerge from this analysis is the fact that the prestige score of the first job, rather than its wages, appears to provide the motivation for men to change jobs, although wages would

TABLE 4.5 MEAN OCCUPATIONAL PRESTIGE AND WAGES ONE AND TWO YEARS
AFTER ENTRY, BY NUMBER OF JOBS HELD IN THE FIRST YEAR
AND IN THE FIRST TWO YEARS AFTER ENTRY, BY RACE

Number of Jobs Held	Mean Occupational Prestige One Year after Entry		Mean Wages One Year after Entry ($/month)	
	White	Black	White	Black
Jobs in the first year after entry				
One	29.7	25.2	248	206
Two or more	31.9	26.6	286	244
Two	32.0	26.7	292	245
Three	32.2	26.3	270	240
Four or more	30.1	16.3†	255	275†
Total	30.5	25.5	261	214
Percent of variance explained by number of jobs	.8	.6	1.7*	1.4
Jobs in the first two years after entry				
One	30.8	25.9	267	211
Two or more	32.4	26.2	311	251
Two	32.5	26.2	291	259
Three	32.1	26.7	303	244
Four	33.1	24.8	376	208
Five or more	31.5	24.2†	472	164
Total	31.7	26.0	293	226
Percent of variance explained by number of jobs	.5	.1	4.4*	2.5*

* Statistically significant at .05
† Less than ten cases

appear to be a more tangible indicator of the benefits of a job. It may be that the starting wage of the job, which is used in this analysis, is not a sufficiently accurate indicator of the rate of pay, since wages can increase in the course of the job. This possibility is explored in the next section.

The comparison of the men who change jobs in the first 2 years with those who do not suggests that there are rewards to increased mobility. The decision to change jobs provides a person with a new opportunity to find a good job, an opportunity that tends to be taken by men with poorer first jobs. It has not so far been shown that the men who change jobs actually succeed in obtaining better jobs. Zeller et al. (1970:35) find that their respondents who change jobs during the 1-year period after entry have poorer first jobs to begin with, but at the end of the year they are still further behind the group of men who have not changed jobs. Over the 1-year period, the wage difference between the "movers" and "stayers" increases from $.20 to $.30 per hour for whites and from $.25 to $.33 per hour for blacks.

Our data display the opposite pattern, the wage gains made by individuals who change jobs are generally *greater* than those obtained by men who remain at their first jobs. Examining the pay rates of whites with 1 year's experience in the labor force, it is found that the mean wages of individuals who hold only one job grow by $13 per month, to $248 per month, compared to an increase of $41, to an average of $292 per month, among men who change jobs. Table 4.5 reveals that the individuals who hold more than one job have higher average wages afer 1 or 2 years in the labor force. A detailed examination of the relative positions of men with two, three, and four or more jobs fails to turn up readily interpretable patterns—after 2 years, whites with more than two jobs have noticeably higher wages than those with only two jobs, but blacks with more than two jobs have rates of pay that fall between those of the groups with one and two jobs.

The prestige scores of men who change jobs at least once either in the first year or in the first 2 years are higher than those who do not change, but the differences are very small: 1.6 prestige points separates the white movers and stayers, for blacks the difference is 1.4 points (see Table 4.5). That the gains made by the movers are greater in the wage than in the prestige dimension is evident from the variances explained by the number of jobs held. At the 2-year point, number of jobs held accounts for 0.5% of the variance in white prestige scores and 4.4% of the variance in white wages; for blacks, the values are 0.1% for prestige and 2.5% for wages.

Men with more education have more jobs in the 2 years after entry, so the fact that men with more jobs have higher wages could simply be a reflection of their higher levels of education. In order to separate these effects, wages were regressed on the two factors, both again measured by groups of dummy variables (see Table 4.6). Most of the zero-order differences remain, although holding education constant lowers the impact of the number of jobs. Compared to the group with only one job over the 2

TABLE 4.6   REGRESSION OF OCCUPATIONAL PRESTIGE AND WAGES TWO YEARS AFTER ENTRY ON NUMBER
            OF JOBS HELD IN THE FIRST TWO YEARS AFTER ENTRY AND EDUCATION TWO YEARS AFTER
            ENTRY, BY RACE

| | Dependent Variable | | | |
| | Occupational Prestige Two Years after Entry | | Wages Two Years after Entry ($/month) | |
Independent Variable or Group of Variables	White	Black	White	Black
REGRESSION COEFFICIENT				
Education**				
Some high school	5.9*	3.1*	67*	65*
High school graduate	7.3*	7.2*	97*	102*
Some college	11.3*	9.8*	153*	202*
College graduate	25.4*	20.7*	233*	206*
Number of jobs held**				
Two	.7	-1.1	10	28
Three	.0	-1.2	17	14
Four	.2	-1.4	78	-8
Five or more	.7	-2.8	203	51
Regression Constant	22.9*	21.9*	180*	150*
PERCENT OF VARIANCE EXPLAINED IN STARTING WAGE OF FIRST JOB				
Zero-order effect				
Education	34.3*	24.0*	13.5*	19.0*
Number of jobs	.5	.1	4.4*	2.5*
Unique effect				
Education	33.9*	24.2*	12.7*	17.4*
Number of jobs	.1	.4	3.6*	.9
Total without interaction	34.4*	24.4*	17.1*	19.9*
Interaction effect	1.4	3.7	8.6	1.8
Total with interaction	35.8*	28.1*	25.7*	21.7*

 * Statistically significant at .05
 ** The four dummy variables for education measure the impact of the levels of education
    relative to the group with no high school. The effect of the number of jobs is re-
    lative to the group with only one job.

years, whites with two jobs average $10 per month more in wages at the
2-year point, those with three jobs are ahead by $17, those with four jobs
gain $78, and those with five or more jobs earn an average of $203 per
month more than those still at the first job. The number of jobs uniquely
explains 3.6% of the variation in wages at the 2-year point. For blacks, it
amounts to only 0.9%. Blacks with two jobs are $28 better off than those
with one, those with three jobs are $14 ahead, and those with four jobs are
$8 per month behind. It is interesting to find that whites who change jobs
tend to reap large wage benefits, while blacks do not. However, this

conclusion is based on a very small number of cases, and its magnitude may be exaggerated.

The number of jobs held during the 2 years after entry has almost no impact on the prestige score of the job held at the conclusion of this period. So, while men who start out with low prestige scores in their first jobs are more likely to change jobs, all they achieve by doing so is to bring themselves up to the average prestige values of men with equal education. The very small differences that are observed are all positive or zero for whites, negative for blacks—but none is statistically significant.

The two parts of this analysis can be summarized in the following way. It is the men with low prestige scores, compared to their fellow respondents of equal education, who are more likely to change jobs in the first year or first 2 years after entry. And they thereby succeed in increasing their prestige scores. Still, the prestige score of the first job is not a very strong predictor of who will change jobs. The movers do not start out with lower wages than those who stay, and after 2 years in the labor force they have slightly higher wages. On the whole, this methodology does not seem a particularly effective way of investigating mobility, in view of the weakness of the patterns discovered. The small magnitudes of differences observed are of considerable significance, and we have certainly been successful in identifying some variables that do not affect mobility. But the problem of determining what *does* explain mobility remains.

AN INTENSIVE ANALYSIS OF THE DURATION OF THE FIRST JOB

Attention has so far been focused on attempting to distinguish the groups of individuals holding different numbers of jobs in the first 2 years after entry, and we have dealt primarily with the differences between men who remain at their first jobs for some period and those who change jobs. This section takes an alternative tack. Instead of looking at the number of jobs held in a specific period, it examines very closely the duration of the first job after entry. By determining the factors that affect the length of time an individual remains at one job, we can infer what it is that makes him want to change jobs. Again, linear regression is used to analyze the simultaneous impacts of a large number of variables. If the analysis of the numbers of jobs held has failed to explain much of the variation in this sort of measure of mobility, the duration variable doesn't seem much more promising. Education, the most powerful predictor of the quality of a job, expalins no more than 5% of the variation in first job duration.

Three groups of variables are used in this regression (see Table 4.7). They describe, first, some characterstics of the respondents; second, the quality of his first job after entry (the one whose duration is the dependent variable); and third, the transition between the first and second job. For the first two groups of variables do temporally precede the duration variable, since the duration of the job is defined by a decision made at the end of that job. But the variables that describe the transition, for example the extent of unemployment between the first and second job, do not unambiguously preceded the duration. We can make the argument that the decision to leave the job—and in more than five out of six cases the respondent reports that he himself made this choice—is partly based on an evaluation of the labor market and of the likelihood of being unemployed. A total of twenty-two variables were used to predict the duration of the first job, measured in months.[4] For convenience, they are described and their means and standard deviations are listed in Table 4.7. The regression is in Table 4.8.

The eight variables describing the respondent measure his educational attainment, age at entry, marital status and the number of children in his own family (not that of his parents). Education is measured by the same four dummy variables as before. It has been shown that men with more education are more mobile; this regression makes it possible to determine how much of this mobility can still be attributed to education when other factors are held constant. Married men and those with children, because of their financial responsibilities, run greater risks than single

---

[4] A small proportion of the sample had no second job after entry, they stayed at the job they obtained after entry until the point at which they were interviewed. Unfortunately we have no real idea of the actual durations of these jobs. It is logical to assume that a job held continuously from the entry point will last considerably beyond the point of the interview—most of the men in this group had held these jobs for 10 or more years. Excluding these men from the population (they constitute 2.6% of the whites and 2.6% of the blacks) would introduce bias into the sample. An arbitrary solution was adopted: the durations of these jobs were doubled, as were the magnitudes of the changes in pay received during the job. This seemed to make sense and yielded a significantly better fit for the regression as a whole; it increased the explained variance by about 10% for whites, 15% for blacks.

TABLE 4.7   VARIABLES USED IN REGRESSION ANALYSIS OF THE DURATION OF FIRST JOB AFTER ENTRY

Variable	Mean or Proportion		Comments
	White	Black	
Education at entry			Four dummy variables, so no assumption
Some high school	.193	.330	of linearity is necessary; each ef-
High school graduate	.439	.291	fect is measured relative to the
Some college	.083	.053	lowest group with no high school, not
College graduate	.109	.029	relative to the previous group
Age at entry	18.3	17.3	In years
Marital status	.177	.214	Dummy variable
Number of children	.02	.03	Few respondents had any children, of those who did, almost all had one child
Level of the first job			
Occupational prestige	29.1	23.8	
Starting wages	243	200	Both wage values in $1959/month
Increase in wages	45	41	
Leaving the first job			Three dummy variables, all with large
Involuntary separation	.123	.156	numbers of missing values; they com-
Had new job	.382	.276	pare men who themselves decided to
Knew of new job	.169	.174	leave the first job to those who were laid off or fired, and men with no new job in mind to those who had a new job or knew of one when they left the first job
Finding the second job			Three dummy variables, and the dis-
Direct method	.411	.426	tance moved in miles (zero for non-
Promotion	.117	.058	movers); compares men who located
Geographic move	.113	.162	their first job through family or
Distance of move	59.0	65.2	friends to all others, and men who moved between the first and second jobs to those who did not
Unemployment between jobs			Two variables are used, one a dummy,
Any unemployment	.116	.164	to represent the potentially non-
Length	.113	.173	linear relationship to duration; length is in months
Second job in military	.264	.201	Dummy variable
Mobility between jobs			
Occupational prestige	2.4	2.4	
Wages	33	41	In $1959/month
Duration of the first Job	23.2	40.4	In months

men when they change jobs—suggesting that they should have longer first job durations. Three measures of the quality of the first job, its occupational prestige score, the wage at the start of the job, and the change in wages *during* the job, are entered in the regression. All three of these variables, including the change in wages, temporally preceded the duration of the first job—since the decision to leave the first job is based on the rate

TABLE   4.8   REGRESSION OF DURATION OF FIRST JOB AFTER ENTRY OF MANY
              VARIABLES, BY RACE, FOR MEN WITH FIRST JOBS IN THE CIVILIAN
              LABOR FORCE

Independent Variable	Regression Coefficient		Standardized Regression Coefficient		Percent of Variance Explained by Group at Unique Levels (zero-order levels in parentheses)	
	White	Black	White	Black	White	Black
Education at entry						
Some high school	-13.4	-9.2	-.095*	.063	.6	1.3
High school graduate	-16.8	-12.9	-.150*	-.085†	(1.0)	(2.5)
Some college	-20.2	-42.2	-.100	-.138*		
College graduate	-28.8	-11.1	-.160	-.027		
Age at entry	-1.45	-4.30	-.071	-.142*	.1	.8
					(.0)	(.8)
Marital status	14.3	29.0	.098*	.172*	.7	2.6
Number of children	2.4	11.3	.008	.049	(10.6)	(13.8)
Level of first job						
Occupational prestige	.765	-.653	.181*	-.089†	45.2	43.6
Starting wages	.012	.089	.029	.156*	52.8	(48.3)
Increase in wages	.219	.490	.696*	.815*		
Leaving the first job						
Involuntary separation	-11.0	4.7	-.066†	.025	1.0	.2
Had new job	-3.4	-12.1	-.030	-.059*	(2.3)	(.8)
Knew of new job	10.4	-8.5	.071*	-.025		
Finding the second job						
Direct method	-8.4	-14.4	-.074*	-.103	.5	1.4
Promotion	-.2	6.2	-.001	.021	(2.8)	(3.4)
Geographic move	-.7	-2.9	-.004	-.016		
Distance of move	-.000	-.010	-.001	.032		
Unemployment between jobs						
Any unemployment	-14.5	-11.7	-.083*	-.086*	1.1	.3
Length	-.40	.21	-.046	.026	(1.6)	(.7)
Second job in the military	-7.7	2.6	-.061†	.015	.3	.1
					(1.2)	(2.0)
Mobility between jobs						
Occupational prestige	.066	-.067	.146*	-.096*	3.5	8.7
Wages	.062	.019	.158*	.400*	(3.0)	(.0)
Regression constant	35.3	94.5				
Percent of variance explained by all variables	63.2	64.8				

* Statistically significant at .01
† Statistically significant at .05

of pay at the moment when the respondent decides to seek other employment, that is, at the end of the job.

Dummy variables are used to indicate whether the respondent leaves his first job voluntarily or involuntarily—either because he is laid off or because he is fired—and to show whether or not he already knew of or had acquired a second job at the time of leaving the first one. The method used to find the second job is classified into the three customary categories: reliance on family and friends, use of "active" means, and promotion. Two variables show whether or not the respondent moves geographically between the first and second jobs and the distance of these moves (zero for nonmovers). Two variables measure the length of time that the respondent is unemployed after the first job. The regression also includes a variable indicating whether the second job is in the armed forces—if the military draft has the effect of pulling men out of their first jobs, the men with second jobs in the military should have shorter first jobs. The change in occupational prestige and wages between the end of the first job and the start of the next job are also entered in the regression. Only men whose first jobs are not in the armed forces are included in the regression. (Men in the military had to spend at least 2 years in service, and this period could be extended only in fixed intervals, so their situation is not comparable to that of men in the civilian labor force.) Separate regressions are performed for whites and blacks.

These variables explain a remarkably large proportion of the variance in duration of the first job: 63.2% for whites and 64.8% for blacks. This is a very high level of prediction; by comparison, a regression with about an equal number of variables explained only 35% of the variance in the prestige score of the first job and about one-half as much of the variance in its wages. Since the ordering of some of the independent variables is not clear, it is possible to place only approximate limits on the variances explained by the three groups of independent variables. The group of variables measuring the respondent's age, education, marital status, and number of children account for between 5% and 15% of the variance in the duration; the prestige score and wages of the first job account for between 40% and 50% of the variance; and the variables describing the transition between the first and the second jobs account for the remaining 10%. These estimates hold for both races. Approximately one-third of the variance remains unexplained. The great predictive power of this method provides the basis for a qualitatively better understanding of the process of occupational mobility than did our examination, in the section above, of the impact of the number of jobs held, where the explained variances were of the order of 2% or 3%. This regression demonstrates that the critical factor in the decision to leave a job is the nature of the job itself and not such personal characteristics of the respondent as his education or marital status, although these play some part. Thus the fundamental dynamic is situational, it involves an evaluation of the job by the respondent.

There is a remarkable resemblance between the results obtained for blacks and whites in the two regressions, as shown in Table 4.8. The mechanisms explaining durations of first jobs do not differ, as the similarity of explained variances and *standardized* regression coefficients shows; but the parameters of the actual process, the *unstandardized* regression coefficients, do vary, because the distributions of many of the variables, and hence their variances are not the same for whites and blacks. Let us now examine each of the variables in the regression in turn.

1. *Education at Entry into the Labor Force.* With all the other variables held constant, education uniquely explains just 0.6% of the variation in the duration of the first job for whites and 1.3% for blacks, compared to zero-order effects amounting to 1.0% for whites and 2.5% blacks. For whites, each increase in the level of education brings a *decrease* in the duration; respondents with some high school spend an average of 13.4 fewer months on the first job than those with no high school; high school graduates average 16.8 months less, men with some college 20.2 months less, and college graduates 28.2 months less than the group with no high school. For blacks, the results are quite similar, except that college graduates' first job durations fall midway between those of respondents with some high school and high school graduates. Blacks with some college average a remarkable 42.2 months less time at the first job than blacks with no high school. This ranking is somewhat different than that obtained at the zero-order level (see Table 3.1). Two important racial differences emerge. Education has more impact on job duration, and hence on mobility, for blacks; second, there is an unusually low level of mobility among black college graduates—suggesting that they suffer particular handicaps in finding good jobs.

2. *Age at Entry into the Labor Force.* Men who enter the labor force when they are older tend to remain at their first jobs for somewhat

shorter periods of time. This lends support to the theory that men with greater skills and resources are more mobile—presuming that chronological age is correlated with increasing maturity and resources. Each additional year of age produces a decline in first job duration of about 4 months for blacks, 1½ months for whites. This variable uniquely explains 0.8% of the variance in first job duration for blacks, an insignificant 0.1% for whites.

3. *Family Composition.* Married men and those with children are likely to stay at their first jobs for longer periods. When the first job duration is regressed on these two variables alone, they explain 10.6% of the variance for whites, 13.8% for blacks. But in the multiple regression, the two unique effects are only 0.8% of the variance for whites and 2.6% of the variance for blacks. These effects are mostly attributable to the marital status variable—married black men have first job durations averaging 29 months longer than those of unmarried blacks; for whites the difference is 14 months. Where there are children—most of the respondents with children have only one child—they add 11.3 months to first job durations of whites, only 2.4 months in the case of blacks.

4. *Level of First Job.* The three variables describing the quality of the first job are by far the strongest of the predictors of first job duration, they *uniquely* explain 45.2% of the variance for whites, 43.6% for blacks. One variable, the change in wage during the first job, accounts for almost all of this effect—41.9% for whites and 42.8% for blacks. For each $10 per month increase in wages, the first job is prolonged by 2 months for whites and by 5 months for blacks. Blacks obtain an average wage increase of $41.4 per month during this job, compared to $45.4 for whites (all values are in 1959 dollars). The zero-order and unique effects of this variable are very similar, since it is not strongly correlated with *any* of the other variables in the regression; for example, educational attainment explains less than 2% of the variance in the *change* in wage during the first job (though of course it accounts for much more of the variance in *starting* wage and prestige score of the job). What is important is that wage increases of equal magnitude produce about *two and one-half* times the increase in job duration for blacks that they do for whites. This suggests that the nature of job market conditions enables employers to maintain the allegiance of a black worker at far less cost than for the equivalent white worker.

In contrast, the effects of prestige score and starting wage of the first job are very small. Whites with higher prestige jobs and blacks with higher

starting wages do have longer first jobs—to the extent of 0.8 of a month
for each prestige point and .9 of a month for each $10 additional starting
salary—but their unique variances are only about 1%. The other two
effects, those of starting wage for whites and prestige score for blacks, are
small, though we should note that blacks with *lower* prestige scores and
higher starting wages have longer first jobs. There is one important conclusion, the predominant factor in determining first job duration is the
amount of wage increase during the job. The fact that the prestige score of
the first job has so little effect on the decision to change jobs suggests that
gains on this measure are very difficult for the average worker to obtain
and that he consequently tends to settle for higher wages.

5. *Leaving the First Job.* The three dummy variables recording
whether or not the first job was terminated involuntarily and whether or
not the respondent had or knew of a second job before leaving the first
one have relatively little impact on duration. Whites who were fired or laid
off from their first jobs have shorter than normal durations, but there is no
difference for blacks. Whites who knew of a second job have longer
durations, but blacks who had a second job at the termination of the first
one have shorter first jobs.[5]

These small and seemingly contradictory effects might be explained
partly by the large number of missing cases among all of these variables.
While approximately one-half of the population knew of or had a second
job at the time they left the first one, only 11.6% of the whites and a
slightly larger proportion of the blacks experienced a month or more of
unemployment between the two jobs, so it appears that most men had
little difficulty finding another job, even if they had no specific knowledge
of new openings beforehand.

6. *Finding the Second Job.* Only one of the four variables in this
group has a significant impact on the duration of the first job. Men who
locate their second jobs by "active" means, that is through advertisements,
employment agencies, or direct application, have shorter first jobs. A fairly

[5] We find that 12.3% of the whites and 15.6% of the blacks report that they
left their first jobs involuntarily—though the proportion of missing cases, 11% for
whites and 12% for blacks, is unusually high. Parnes *et al.* (1970:109) find that 23%
of their sample left their first jobs involuntarily. The very large proportion of missing
cases for the variables measuring whether or not the respondent had or knew of a
new job, 29% for whites and 19% for blacks, makes the estimates of their effects very
unreliable.

large number of individuals find their jobs in this way, about four in ten for both races. The difference in first job duration between this group and those whose jobs were located with the help of their families or friends amounts to 8.4 months for whites and 14.4 months for blacks. Individuals who display more drive in finding a new job are more mobile, as the previous regression analysis of the number of jobs (Table 4.1) also shows. Finding jobs by promotion, making a geographic move between jobs, and the distance of such a move all have negligible effects on job duration. This group of four variables uniquely explains 0.5% of the variation in job duration for whites, 1.4% for blacks.

7. *Unemployment between the First and Second Job.* Only one in six blacks and one in nine whites is unemployed for 1 month or more between the first and second job. There is clear evidence that the men who experience some unemployment leave their first jobs earlier, by 14.5 months for whites and 11.7 months for blacks, than men with comparable characteristics who spend less than one month without work. This suggests that these men had, in effect, left their first jobs "prematurely." The two variables uniquely explain 1.1% of the variance for whites and 0.3% for blacks. It is only the dummy variable indicating whether or not the individual experienced *any* unemployment that has a significant effect, the variable indicating the *length* of the period of unemployment has no significant effect.

8. *Second Job in the Military.* Whites whose second jobs are in the armed forces have first jobs that average 7.7 months less in duration than those of men with civilian jobs. The military draft, or enlistment in the face of the draft, causes whites to leave their first jobs earlier than usual. However, it explains only 0.3% of the variance for whites, and for blacks there is no effect at all.

9. *Changes in Wages and Prestige Scores between the First and Second Job.* Whites gain an average of 2.4 prestige points and $32.8 per month when they change jobs, compared to increments of 2.4 points and $40.7 for blacks. The values of these two variables are strongly related to the duration of the first job, and they uniquely explain 3.5% of its variation for whites and 8.7% for blacks. Men who obtain greater gains in this job transition apparently remain longer in their first jobs waiting for the opportunity of a better second job. Once more, wage changes have a greater impact on job durations than do prestige differences. Holding all other factors constant, each additional month on the job results in a $16 per

month wage increase for whites; for blacks the corresponding increase is $5 per month. This wage increase uniquely explains 7.4% of the variance in first job duration for blacks, only 1.9% for whites.

An inspection of the correlation matrices used to perform the regressions reveals that blacks face a considerable barrier to making wage gains in the period just after they enter the labor force. The increase in wages obtained by changing jobs is *negatively* correlated both with the starting wage of the first job ($r = -.567$) and with the pay increase *during* the first job ($r = -.396$). These relationships have very much the appearance of regression toward the mean, though this is not really what is taking place. The negative correlations simply indicate that blacks who maximize their wage gains at one point are likely to encounter great difficulty in making gains at other times. Because the corresponding correlations for whites, which have the values $-.374$ and $-.004$, are far *smaller*, the possibilities of their making wage gains during the first job and by changing from the first to the second job are much greater.

Blacks with longer first jobs suffer prestige losses in the transition from the first to the second job, at the rate of .067 prestige points per month of duration. In staying at their first jobs for longer periods to obtain larger pay increases, blacks end up with lowered occupational prestige scores. For whites, longer first job durations are positively associated with pay *and* prestige increases (by .066 prestige points per month), while blacks appear to trade prestige for wages. The unique variances associated with this variable are small, 1.1% for whites and 0.5% for blacks—the larger value for whites is a further indication of the more important role that job prestige plays for whites.

The presentation has included a perhaps bewildering array of variables. It is possible to account for 90% of the explained variance in the duration of the first job with only four variables. The four "best" variables explain 58.2% of a total of 63.2% of the variance for whites and 59.6% out of a total of 64.8% of the variance for blacks. These smaller regressions are presented in Table 4.9. Of the four variables with the most explanatory power, three of them—change in wage during the first job, change in wage between the first and second job, and marital status—are common to the regressions for both races. They are respectively the first, second, and fourth variables to enter the equation using a stepwise procedure (forward selection only). For whites, the third variable is the unemployment dummy variable,

TABLE 4.9 REGRESSION OF DURATION OF FIRST JOB AFTER ENTRY ON THE FOUR VARIABLES EXPLAINED NINETY PERCENT OF THE VARIATION ACCOUNTED FOR IN THE LARGER REGRESSION (TABLE 4.8), BY RACE, FOR MEN WITH FIRST JOBS IN THE CIVILIAN LABOR FORCE

Independent Variable	Regression Coefficient		Standardized Regression Coefficient		Simple Correlation	
	White	Black	White	Black	White	Black
Wage increase during the first job	.220	.455	.697	.757	.721	.674
Wage increase between jobs	.072	.149	.184	.310	.174	.004
Unemployed one month or more	-19.2		-.111		-.125	
Age at entry		-5.14		-.183		-.091
Marital status	15.3	32.0	.105	.191	.323	.357
Regression constant	10.4	91.9				
Percent of variance explained	58.2	59.6				

and for blacks it is age at entry. The change in wage during the first job uniquely explains 44.4% of the variance for whites and 44.2% for blacks. The regression coefficients in this regression are very similar to those obtained above. Also, there is very little overlap among the four variables, partly because of the way in which the forward selection procedure makes the choice of variables.

SUMMARY

This analysis has provided clear answers to the three questions posed at the start. First, we have shown that only to a limited extent do individuals exhibit "styles" that lead to their holding jobs for longer or shorter periods. While weak patterns are found, they account for only a small part of the variance in the rates of job mobility in the first years after men enter the labor force. Whites are more mobile than blacks, men with more education generally are more mobile than those with less, and married men are less mobile than single men—but in absolute terms, these variables are quite weak predictors of the extent of job mobility.

As to why men change jobs in these early years of work, the answer is, mainly for monetary reasons. The remarkable power of the wage variable as predictors of the duration of the first job makes it apparent that our respondents behave like "economic men." The relative unimportance of occupational prestige—a good measure of the general desirability of a job—suggests either that men do not think it is as important to increase prestige as wages or that they find it difficult to locate jobs with higher prestige scores, given their level of education. It may also be that this *general* measure of the standing of a job is a relatively poor indication of how a man is likely to be treated at a specific job in a particular firm.

A man whose first job has a lower prestige score than that of the average person with the same education is more likely to change jobs in the first 2 years after entry, and by the point 2 years after entry such men have prestige scores that do not differ significantly from those of the men who have not changed jobs. Although individuals with lower first job wages are no more likely to change jobs, the men who do so have somewhat higher wage rates at the point 2 years after entry. It is found that the black respondents who change jobs are in relatively worse positions than the comparative whites who do so. This finding is another indication of the generally lower mobility rates of blacks observed in the previous chapter.

The fact that we were much more successful in predicting the duration of the first job than whether or not a respondent would change jobs in the first 2 years after entry is the result partly of the difference in the time spans involved, and partly of differences in the methodologies employed. The mean duration of the first job is about 2 years for whites and 3 years for blacks—so in predicting the length of the first job we are dealing with significant numbers of cases in which the duration is several years. To increase the accuracy of prediction requires us to examine a longer period in the careers of some men, though of course quite large numbers of men change jobs in the first couple of years after entry. By confining the investigation to a fixed 2-year interval, it becomes much more difficult to obtain systematic differences and to discover what it is that makes men change jobs. Racial differences emerge at several points in our discussion; there is clear evidence of discrimination, the impact of which is independent of the educational handicaps suffered by blacks. Employers can get more out of blacks than out of whites, for the same money. This is perhaps best illustrated by our finding that a given pay raise will prolong the job tenure of a black worker by a factor two and one-half times greater than that for a white man, comparing whites and blacks with equal levels of education in similar situations. This clearly works to the advantage of the employer of black labor; it suggests that white and black employees are in very different positions when it comes to finding new and better job opportunities—the very much smaller returns to blacks from higher levels of job mobility point in this direction too.

The novelty and intrinsic interest of these results suggests that an orientation toward the study of the micro-processes of occupational mobility could do a great deal to fill in the gaps left by studies of net mobility over longer periods. By focusing in detail on individual elements of work experience it has been possible to bring to light a number of aspects of the mobility processes hidden in studies that span longer periods of time.

The Consequences of Entry 5

So far, this monograph has been concerned with describing the way in which entry into the labor force occurs; this chapter assesses its impact on the subsequent careers of our respondents. As we observed in our review of the literature, Blau and Duncan (1967) present convincing evidence that the socioeconomic score of the first job after entry influences that of later jobs, *independent* of the respondent's education and family background. Our very detailed longitudinal records of work and educational experiences make it possible to develop models of the impact of entry that include both occupational prestige and wages, and in which educational attainment is not fixed at the point immediately preceding entry into the labor force, but changes with time.

As a first step, it is necessary to choose the point at which these occupational outcomes are to be examined, so that the dependent variables can be specified. The analysis begins with an examination of changes in *educational attainment* after entry into the labor force, first describing the nature of these changes and the manner in which they affect the relative standing of whites and blacks, and then using multiple regression to determine what factors are associated with the gains which do take place.

Our second major focus is on *occupational achievement* in the years after entry into the labor force. After describing the extent of both wage and prestige mobility of blacks and whites at each level of education, we assess the impact of the first job after entry on later occupational achievement.

130

The extent of prestige and wage mobility in the period after entry is examined in great detail. First we describe the levels of mobility for whites and blacks in each of the five main educational cateogries. Then the effects of the prestige scores and wages of the first job and of the jobs at the points 1 and 2 years after entry are brought into the analysis. The third step is to take the prestige score and starting wage of the first job and combine these with eleven other variables—measuring the industry of the first job, the method used to locate that job, the respondent's marital status, and whether he moved—in a multiple regression analysis of later achievement. Of course, the respondent's education, family background, and pre-entry jobs are also held constant. Finally a path analysis is used to present, in schematic fashion, the whole of this stratification process.

About one-half of the respondents serve in the armed forces, usually for 2 or 3 years. So, simply in terms of the time spent in military service, it represents an important part of the work experience of these young men. Our data make it possible to carry out a highly detailed analysis of the impact of military service on subsequent careers, an analysis which controls for education, family background, and other variables that might obscure the relationship between military service and later occupational achievement. In addition, we explore the extent to which veterans might make educational gains, comparing them to men of similar characteristics who do not serve.

What constitutes a meaningful measure of the occupational success of our respondents? The main criterion is that the point at which the outcome is measured should be spaced far enough away from the time at which the men entered the labor force to give some realistic indication of later occupational achievement. The principal limitation is imposed by the age composition of the sample; the men are between 30 and 39 years of age at the time of the interview. There are two ways of defining these outcomes; one is to take the job each man holds at a specific age and the second is to select the job he holds a fixed number of years after entry. The former alternative compares respondents of the same age, while the latter controls the amount of labor force experience each man has had. We chose the second of these, preferring to equalize the time in which individuals had the opportunity for occupational mobility. The point 10 years after entry seemed a convenient choice, but it did not prove feasible because approximately one-third of the college graduates in the sample were interviewed at a point before they had accumulated 10 years experience in the work force. Choosing the 10-year interval biases the results by requiring the inclusion of sizeable numbers of college graduates without a full 10 years of work experience or else the extrapolation of the careers of these respondents. By taking the point 8 years after entry, it is possible to reduce the number of men with less than that amount of labor force experience to a small proportion of the total.

Some respondents do not have jobs at the point exactly 8 years after entry; some have temporarily dropped out of the labor force at this point to return to school, others are suffering from illness, or are not looking for work. However, most of those without jobs are unemployed and looking for work. The group without jobs is fairly large, comprising 9.9% of the whites and 8.3% of the blacks. Even at the 8-year point, a small number of college graduates have not experienced 8 years in the labor force. For all these individuals with no jobs at the 8-year point, the job held closest to the point 8 years after entry is used in the analysis.[1] This substitution defines the outcome variables for the entire sample, and so prevents the potentially biasing effect of nonrandomness among the missing cases while slightly cutting down on random error by increasing the number of cases in the analysis.

EDUCATIONAL ATTAINMENT 8 YEARS AFTER ENTRY

In the 8 years following entry, 26.8% of the white respondents and 11.6% of the black respondents experience some educational mobility, as far as it can be measured on the 10-point scale of education (see Table 5.1). The educational gains are very unequally distributed. Men who enter the labor force with the least education also make the smallest gains; only 11 of the 132 whites and 1 of the 184 blacks in this category obtain at least some high school. The proportion of men with some high school declines, while the proportion of high school graduates remains approximately constant—the inflow of new high school graduates being equal to the outflow, that is, to the proportion of high school graduates who obtain

---

[1] About one-half of the jobs substituted fall within 6 months of the exact 8-year point, another one-third are between 7 and 24 months away, while the remainder, for about 2% of the total sample, are more than 2 years from the point 8 years after entry.

TABLE 5.1 DISTRIBUTION OF EDUCATION AT ENTRY AND EIGHT YEARS AFTER ENTRY AND OF CHANGES IN EDUCATION, BY RACE

Race and Education	Distribution (percent)		Changes in Education in the Eight Years after Entry (as a percent of the number at that level at entry)						
	At Entry	Eight Years after Entry	No Change	Within a Major Category	Some High School	High School Graduate	Some College	College Graduate	Total
White									
No high school	15.5	14.2	88.6	2.6	2.9	5.2	.0	.7	100.0
Some high school	21.0	15.7	72.1	.0		22.9	5.0	.0	100.0
High school graduate	42.9	42.9	66.0	21.8			8.5	4.7	100.0
Some college	9.8	11.5	71.1	.0				28.9	100.0
College graduate	10.7	15.7	83.5	16.5					100.0
Total, percent	100.0	100.0	73.2	26.8	.5	5.6	4.7	4.9	100.0
Number of cases	850	850							
Black									
No high school	24.9	24.8	99.5	.5	.0		.0	.0	100.0
Some high school	35.2	31.3	88.5	.0		11.1	.0	.4	100.0
High school graduate	30.0	31.7	77.9	14.8			5.5	1.8	100.0
Some college	6.5	7.9	95.8	.0				4.2	100.0
College graduate	3.4	4.3	84.0	16.0					100.0
Total, percent	100.0	100.0	88.4	5.1	.1	3.9	1.6	.9	100.0
Number of cases	738	738							

at least some college. The proportion of men with some college increases from 9.9% to 11.6% for whites and from 6.5% to 7.9% for blacks. The number of white college graduates rises by almost one-half in these 8 years, from 10.7% to 15.6% of the sample, the increase in the proportion of black college graduates is from 3.4% to 4.3%.

Scoring education on the 10-point scale, the correlations between educational attainment at entry and 8 years later are very large, amounting to .898 for whites and .945 for blacks. The gap between whites and blacks widens during this period, from .86 to .97 units. The average levels of education rise by half a unit to a level above high school graduate for whites, and by a third of a unit to a point midway between "some high school" and "high school graduate" for blacks. It is clear that the amount of education with which a person enters the labor force is a very powerful predictor of his educational level 8 years later, but the correlation between his education at entry and the *change* during this period is virtually zero for whites ($r = .007$), and small for blacks ($r = .162$).

Some of the educational gains made are more important than others. For whites, 58.6% of the men who make some such gain move to a higher category of educational level, and for blacks the proportion is nearly the same, 56.0% of the total. The remainder of the educational mobility involves less important changes, such as obtaining some additional elementary schooling, but not graduating.

Though our conclusions about specific educational transitions are based on a small number of cases, the outlines of the process are clear. Most of the "transitions," even considering only the ones that cross the boundaries separating the five main categories, move the individuals up only one step on the scale. Thus, 23% of the whites who enter with some high school are high school graduates 8 years later, 5% graduate from high school, and 5% obtain some college, but not one graduates from college. Of the 34% of the white high school graduates who gain some additional schooling after entry, 20% obtain some vocational training, 9% complete some college, and 5% graduate from college. This pattern is even more marked for blacks. Of the 13% of whites who rise from the category of high school graduates, about two-thirds obtain some college and one-third graduate from college; of the 7% of black high school graduates who obtain more education, about one-quarter graduate from college. The changes in educational attainment after entry are much more unequally divided between blacks and whites than is the education with which they

TABLE 5.2   REGRESSION OF EDUCATION EIGHT YEARS AFTER ENTRY AND OF CHANGES
            IN EDUCATION, BY RACE

Independent Variable	Regression Coefficient		Standardized Regression Coefficient		Simple Correlation with Dependent Variable	
	White	Black	White	Black	White	Black
Family background						
Father's education	.035	.035	.037	.036†	.417	.330
Mother's education	-.022	.001	-.020	.001	.376	.356
Father's occupation	-.021	.029	-.033†	.071*	-.338	-.156
Number of siblings	.005	-.001	.032	-.012	.373	.241
Education at entry	.895	.975	.841*	.957*	.898	.945
Number of jobs before entry						
Full-time	.010	-.035	.012	-.027†	.533	.237
Part-time	.010	.026	.010	.019	.361	.230
Level of first job						
Prestige score	.0018	.0095	.012	.053*	.475	.380
Starting wages	.00035	-.00092	.025	-.069*	.380	.279
Military service	.22	.04	.057*	.013	.054	.338
Regression constant	.48	.18				

* Statistically significant at .01
† Statistically significant at .05

enter the labor force. The larger implication is that entry into the labor
force, as it has been defined here, marks a more definitive break between
education and the work world for blacks than it does for whites.

The multiple regression shown in Table 5.2, with variance estimates
in Table 5.3, shows which respondents are more likely to acquire additional education during the 8 years after entry. Educational attainment at
this point was regressed on family background, education at entry, pre-
entry jobs, prestige scores and wages at the start of the first job, and a
dummy variable indicating whether or not the respondent had served in
the armed forces at any time during his first 8 years in the labor force. The
total variance explained by these ten variables is impressively high, 81.4%
for whites and 90.5% for blacks—the greater black variance reflecting their
lower degree of educational mobility during this time. On closer examination, however, it is apparent that these variables are almost completely

TABLE 5.3 PROPORTION OF VARIANCE EXPLAINED IN REGRESSION ANALYSIS OF EDUCATION EIGHT YEARS AFTER ENTRY BY FIVE VARIABLES, BY RACE

| Dependent Variable and Group of Independent Variables | Percent of Variance Explained | | | | | | | |
| | White | | | | Black | | | |
	Zero-Order	Unique	Addi-tional	Cumu-lative	Zero-Order	Unique	Addi-tional	Cumu-lative
Occupational prestige of first job								
Family background	26.8	0.3	26.8	26.8	15.4	.4	15.4	15.4
Education at entry	80.6	30.3	54.3	81.1	89.4	55.7	74.5	89.9
Number of jobs before entry	31.1	.0	0.0	81.1	7.9	.0	0.1	89.9
First job	28.9	.0	0.0	81.1	18.5	.5	0.6	90.5
Military service	0.3	0.3	0.3	81.4	11.5	.0	0.0	90.5

incapable of predicting educational *mobility*; the most important result from the regression is rather trivial—level of education at entry *alone* can account for about 99% of the variance explained by the entire group of variables. It explains 80.6% of the variance for whites, a value which increases by only .8% with the remaining nine variables. If we also control for family background, the additional variance drops to only 0.3%. In other words, educational level at entry leaves 19.4% of the variance in education after entry *unexplained*, and the other variables are able to account for only about one-twentieth of this remainder. For blacks, education at entry explains 89.4% of the final educational level, and the remaining variables add only 1.1%. So, while it is possible to predict educational level 8 years after entry with very great accuracy, we are almost completely incapable of explaining educational *mobility*.

Inserting the groups of variables in the temporal order in which they occur, for whites, family background explains 26.8% of the variation in education 8 years after entry, education at entry adds 54.3%, number of jobs before entry and prestige score and starting wage of the first job have no effect, and military service adds .3% to the variance. For blacks, family background is less important and accounts for 15.4% of the variation, education at entry has a greater effect, 74.5%, number of jobs before entry adds .1%, prestige score and starting wage of first job add .6%, and military service has no effect.

A number of small but interesting effects appear in the regressions. For example, blacks whose fathers have more education or occupations with higher prestige scores are more likely to gain education; but, for whites, three measures of a "better" family background—higher values for mother's education and father's occupation and *fewer* siblings—all *lower* educational attainment at the 8-year point (though father's education does exert a smaller countereffect). Blacks with more full-time jobs before entry gain less education, though there is a positive relationship between the number of part-time jobs and education. Also blacks with higher prestige scores at entry and *lower* starting wages obtain more education. This small but statistically significant effect suggests that blacks who chose to take first jobs with higher prestige scores but lower wages are also more likely to make efforts to get more schooling. Whites with more pre-entry jobs and higher first job prestige scores *and* wages gain very small amounts of education. Veterans gain slightly more education than non-veterans during the 8 years, to the extent of .22 units for whites and a negligible

.04 units for blacks. While these results are suggestive and a much larger sample might tell us more about them, their net impact of these variables on educational mobility is marginal.

PRESTIGE SCORES, WAGES, AND NUMBER OF JOBS HELD 8 YEARS AFTER ENTRY

As shown in Table 5.4, the average prestige score of the first job, for whites, is 29.3 points, a value that increases to 37.1 in the 8 years after entry. For blacks, the increase is from 24.8 at entry to 28.5 points. So the gap between the races almost doubles, from 4.5 to 8.6 points, in the space of 8 years. Though whites and blacks at each level of education make gains during this period, some groups gain far more than others. For blacks, the mean prestige score of those with no high school at entry rises by only 1.0 prestige points over the 8 years, compared to gains of 3.7 points for high school graduates and 10.2 points for college graduates. The corresponding figures for whites are 4.6, 7.8, and 9.1 prestige points. Whites at or below high school graduation level at entry, make far larger prestige gains than comparable blacks—the result being that the small racial differences at entry grow significantly. For example, whites with some high school gain 6.0 prestige points, compared to only 1.8 points for their black counterparts. However, the gap between white and black college graduates falls from 7.5 to 6.5 points.

A somewhat similar pattern appears in the tabulation of wage statistics. At each of the five levels of education, the mean wages of whites increase more than those of blacks; among the men with least education, this difference grows from $7 per month for the first job to $56 per month for the job held at the 8-year point. In general, the size of the mean wage gains over the 8 years varies directly with the level of education. Whites with no high school gain $164 per month, white high school graduates gain $196, and white college graduates gain $273 per month. However the *ratios* of wages among the levels of education do not change much; college graduates earn about twice as much and high school graduates about one and one-half times as much as men with no high school.

In the 8 years after entry into the labor force, the average respondent changes jobs two or three times, though there is wide variation in the

TABLE 5.4 NUMBER OF JOBS HELD IN THE EIGHT YEARS AFTER ENTRY, BY EDUCATION EIGHT YEARS AFTER ENTRY AND RACE

Race and Education Eight Years after Entry	Occupational Prestige				Wages ($/month)			
	First Job	Eight Years after Entry	Difference	Percent Increase	First Job	Eight Years after Entry	Difference	Percent Increase
White								
No high school	22.7	27.3	4.6	20	149	313	164	110
Some high school	26.5	32.5	6.0	23	230	381	151	66
High school graduate	28.3	36.1	7.8	28	249	445	196	79
Some college	32.7	41.0	8.3	25	272	494	222	82
College graduate	46.0	55.1	9.1	20	354	627	273	77
Total	29.3	37.1	7.8	27	243	455	212	87
Missing values (percent)								
In armed forces	.7				16.8	7.3		
Other		.2			10.5	10.1		
Total number of cases	850	850			850	850		
Black								
No high school	21.4	22.4	1.0	5	142	257	115	81
Some high school	23.9	25.7	1.8	8	200	341	141	70
High school graduate	26.0	29.7	3.7	14	222	388	166	75
Some college	29.9	36.0	6.1	20	281	438	157	66
College graduate	38.5	48.6	10.1	26	294	528	234	80
Total	24.8	28.5	3.7	15	200	357	157	53
Missing values (percent)								
In armed forces	.3				16.3	8.5		
Other		.0			12.5	7.3		
Total number of cases	738	738			738	738		

number of jobs held (see Table 5.5). There are no large differences among
the categories of education or between whites and blacks, but two trends
are apparent: Whites are more likely to switch jobs; and the relationship
between education and the number of jobs held is curvilinear—white high
school graduates and blacks with some college change jobs most frequently. Something less than one-tenth of the men hold only one job in
this period, two-thirds hold between two and five jobs, about one-fifth
hold six or seven jobs, and one-tenth hold eight or more jobs.

As education increases from no high school to the some college level,
there are steadily decreasing proportions of men still on their first jobs,
though this percentage rises somewhat for college graduates. For whites,
13% of the men with no high school but only 3% of those with some
college are still in their first jobs after 8 years. The corresponding figures
for blacks are 15% of the men with no high school and 2% of those with
some college. Among college graduates, 8% of the whites and 9% of the
blacks are still in their first jobs. The lower rates of job mobility at the
extremes of the educational distribution likely have different causes. The
men with the least education probably have difficulty finding better jobs
to move to, while the college graduates initially obtain good jobs that
make use of their training and thus have less reason to change jobs.

Similar findings emerge from an examination of the number of jobs
held, and they allow easier comparisons of the job mobility of specific
groups. Whites hold an average of 3.6 jobs in the 8 years, compared to 2.8
jobs for blacks. The largest racial differences appear for men with little
education. Whites with no high school average 3.3 jobs in this period,
compared to only 2.4 for blacks. The gap is considerably smaller for the
other groups, so we find that whites with some college average 3.5 jobs in
this period, compared to a mean of 3.2 jobs for blacks with some college.

Population estimates of the effect of education and race on prestige
scores and wages 8 years after entry are again obtained by performing a
dummy variable regression, with the cases weighted to approximate the
ratio of blacks to whites in the U.S. population; the results are shown in
Table 5.6. The race and educational attainment variables explain 41.7% of
the variance in the prestige scores and 23.3% of the variance in wages 8
years after entry.

These regressions yield somewhat different results than the corresponding analyses of the prestige score and starting wage of the first job in
Table 2.11. The most significant change is in the impact of race: The cost

TABLE 5.5 MEAN OCCUPATIONAL PRESTIGE AND WAGES OF FIRST JOB AND EIGHT YEARS AFTER ENTRY AND MEAN INCREASE DURING THE FIRST EIGHT YEARS AFTER ENTRY, BY EDUCATION AT THE TIME AND RACE

Race and Education Eight Years After Entry	Number of Jobs Held in the Eight Years After Entry (Percentage Distribution)						Mean	Standard Deviation	Number of Cases
	1	2-3	4-5	6-7	8 or more	Total			
White									
No high school	13	33	29	14	11	100	3.3	2.9	120
Some high school	6	31	32	22	9	100	3.7	2.7	133
High school graduate	2	25	41	20	12	100	3.9	2.2	365
Some college	3	25	48	16	8	100	3.5	1.9	99
College graduate	8	34	36	14	8	100	3.1	2.0	133
Total	6	28	39	18	9	100	3.6	2.3	850
Black									
No high school	15	45	29	7	4	100	2.4	2.0	183
Some high school	8	37	33	8	4	100	2.8	1.9	231
High school graduate	4	43	37	11	5	100	3.0	1.8	234
Some college	2	36	33	26	3	100	3.2	1.8	58
College graduate	9	34	44	13	0	100	2.6	2.0	32
Total	8	41	37	10	4	100	2.8	1.9	738

TABLE 5.6   REGRESSION OF OCCUPATIONAL PRESTIGE AND WAGES EIGHT YEARS AFTER
ENTRY AND NUMBER OF JOBS HELD IN THE EIGHT YEARS AFTER ENTRY
ON RACE AND EDUCATION EIGHT YEARS AFTER ENTRY AND RACE

Independent Variable or Group of Variables	Dependent Variable		
	Occupational Prestige Eight Years after Entry	Wages Eight Years after Entry ($/month)	Number of Jobs in the Eight Years after Entry
REGRESSION COEFFICIENTS			
Race**	-5.8	-47	-.81
Education eight years after entry**			
5-7 years	4.2	40	1.21
Elementary school graduate	5.3	113	1.23
Some high school	9.1	147	1.42
High school graduate	12.2	206	1.66
High school graduate and some vocational	15.0	217	1.57
Some college	17.9	257	1.28
College graduate	29.3	357	.96
Master's degree	34.0	374	.51
Some graduate or professional	23.0	331	3.36
Graduate or professional degree	44.7	812	.38
Regression constant	23.2	236	2.24
PERCENT OF VARIANCE EXPLAINED			
Zero-order effect			
Race	4.9	1.8	1.2
Education eight years after entry	40.1	23.0	2.8
Unique Effect			
Race	1.6	0.3*	1.1
Education eight years after entry	36.8	21.5	2.7
Common	3.3	1.5	.1
Total without interaction	41.7	23.3	3.9
Interaction effect	.2*	.2*	.2*
Total with interaction	41.9	23.5	4.1

*   Not statistically significant at .05

** Effects measured relative to whites with no high school

of being black (i.e., the difference between whites and blacks, *holding educational attainment constant*) rises from 2.2 prestige points at entry to 5.8 points after 8 years. The unique variance explained by race also increases from 0.3% at entry to 1.6% at the later point—a rather large proportion, given the fact that only one-ninth of the population is black. The variance explained by both race and education, in eleven categories, increases from 31.6% to 41.7%, with most of this change due to education. The gap between the average prestige scores of whites and blacks is 9.9 prestige points; thus 60% of the difference, or 5.8 points, is due to factors other than education.

The wage regression yields a very similar result; the cost of being black, which amounts to $16 per month at entry, triples to $47 per month in 8 years. This $47 compares to an *average* difference of $98 per month in the wages of whites and blacks. Thus about one-half of the racial wage differential is removed by equalizing education.

During these 8 years following entry, the relationship of education to job prestige grows stronger. Also, education continues to be a better predictor of prestige scores than of wages, and it predicts both of these variables more accurately for whites than for blacks. Educational attainment (in eleven categories) explains 39.5% of the variance in the occupational prestige scores for whites, but only 30.6% for blacks. For the first job after entry, the corresponding values (in Table 2.11) are 31.6% for whites and 19.1% for blacks. By the point 8 years after entry, education explains 22.3% of the variance in wages for whites, 17.4% for blacks. At entry, education accounts for 19.2% of the variance in wages for whites, 12.6% for blacks.

When the number of jobs held in these 8 years is regressed on educational attainment and race—as for the occupational prestige and wage variables—we find that the total explained variance is only 3.9% (this weighted regression is also in Table 5.6). The unique effect of education amounts to 2.7% of the variance, and race uniquely explains 1.1% of the variance. So, in predicting the number of jobs held race plays a relatively more important role than it does for either prestige or wages after 8 years. But neither race nor education has much effect. The same conclusion was reached in the intensive analysis of job mobility in the first 2 years after entry (in Chapter 4), it was found that situational factors have a far greater effect on job changing than do an individual's socioeconomic characteristics. The number of jobs held in the first 2 years after entry has very little

TABLE 5.7 PROPORTION OF VARIANCE IN OCCUPATIONAL PRESTIGE EIGHT YEARS AFTER ENTRY EXPLAINED BY OCCUPATIONAL PRESTIGE OF THE FIRST JOB AND ONE AND TWO YEARS AFTER ENTRY, AND BY EDUCATION AT ENTRY, AND PROPORTION OF VARIANCE IN WAGES EIGHT YEARS AFTER ENTRY EXPLAINED BY STARTING WAGES OF THE FIRST JOB AND ONE AND TWO YEARS AFTER ENTRY, AND BY EDUCATION AT ENTRY, BY RACE

Percent of Variance Explained

Dependent and Independent Variable	Prestige or Wages Alone		Prestige or Wages and Education at Entry		Unique Effect of Prestige or Wages	
	White	Black	White	Black	White	Black
Occupational prestige eight years after entry						
Prestige of first job	21.4	16.9	37.3	32.1	3.5	5.3
Prestige one year after entry	25.2	20.8	38.0	33.3	4.3	6.5
Prestige two years after entry	29.6	20.4	40.4	32.1	6.7	5.3
Wages eight years after entry						
Starting wages of first job	16.4	22.5	27.5	29.9	6.7	12.6
Wages one year after entry	21.6	28.0	30.5	33.0	9.7	15.7
Wages two years after entry	52.5	27.8	57.4	32.1	36.6	14.8

impact on respondents' wages and prestige scores at that point; this continues to be true at the point 8 years after entry. The prestige score and wages 8 years after entry were regressed on educational attainment 8 years after entry and on the numbers of jobs held in this period (as in Tables 4.3 and 4.4). The impact of the number of jobs was negligible. The only interesting (though statistically insignificant) finding is that whites who hold one or two jobs and blacks who hold only one job in the 8 years after entry have earnings averaging about $50 per month below the average for men who hold more jobs, holding education constant.

The occupational prestige scores and wages of the jobs held 8 years after entry are strongly related to the corresponding values for the first job and 1 and 2 years after entry. The prestige score of the first job explains 21.4% of the variation in the prestige score after 8 years for whites, 16.9% for blacks. By the point 2 years after entry, these variances increase to 29.6% and 20.4%. With educational attainment held constant, the contributions of these early jobs are substantially weaker, the first job prestige score uniquely explains 3.5% of the variance for whites, 5.3% for blacks. The starting wage of the first job explains 16.4% of the variance in the wage after 8 years for whites, which rises to 52.5% for the wage of the job held 2 years after entry; the corresponding proportions for blacks are 22.5% and 27.8%. The unique effects of the earlier wage values, with educational attainment held constant, are approximately twice as great as the corresponding estimates for the prestige variable. Wages are more strongly conditioned by earlier wages, while prestige scores are more closely tied to education. So a person's job history is a more meaningful consideration in any analysis of wages.

MILITARY SERVICE IN THE 8 YEARS AFTER ENTRY

Over three-fifths of the white respondents and just under one-half of the black respondents serve in the armed forces during their first 8 years after entry—and because of the age level at this point it is unlikely that many more serve after this time. In this section we will find out which of the respondents served and analyze the impact of military service on subsequent careers. We have already shown that veterans gain slightly more

TABLE 5.8   PROPORTION WITH SOME MILITARY SERVICE IN THE FIRST
            EIGHT YEARS AFTER ENTRY, BY EDUCATION EIGHT YEARS
            AFTER ENTRY AND RACE

| Education Eight Years | Percent Veterans | |
after Entry	White	Black
No high school	38	11
Some high school	59	46
High school graduate	70	68
Some college	71	69
College graduate	53	50
Total	61.2	46.5

education than nonveterans, holding a number of variables constant; in this section we will consider whether they might also gain some other occupational advantage. Browning, Lopreato, and Poston (1973) argue that the armed forces can play the role of a "bridging environment" that provides training and additional education, both during the period of service and in the form of financial aid afterward. They find that Mexican-American and black veterans have higher earnings than their nonveteran counterparts, as do whites in low occupational categories. Unfortunately, the authors do not provide variance estimates to measure the relative importance of military service, nor do they control for education. Cutright (1974) finds the previous evidence inconclusive but obtains relatively small differences himself.

We first compare the prestige scores and wages of veterans and nonveterans, holding race and education constant.[2] In the more complex regression analysis presented in the next section, we will also include variables measuring the impact of military service; but it will not allow us to detect interaction effects, as is possible with the tabular and analysis

---

[2] We leave the question of whether or not civilian earnings forgone during a period of military service are recovered in the course of subsequent careers. Labor economists have been primarily concerned with this problem (see Hansen and Weisbrod 1967; Oi 1967; Miller and Tollison 1971).

of variance methods used here. There is some reason to suspect that the impact of military service might differ according to the individual's educational attainment, on the evidence of Browning, Lopreato, and Poston (1973).

Table 5.8 shows the proportions of men at each of the five levels of educational attainment who serve in the armed forces in the first 8 years after entry. There are no racial differences among those in the three highest educational categories who serve: 70% of high school graduates and those with some college, and 50% of college graudates. Clear differences emerge in the number of whites and blacks with less education who serve: 38% of the whites with no high school, compared to only 11% of the blacks; and, among men with some high school, 59% of the whites versus 46% of the blacks. The large number of blacks in the lowest categories of education, where the race differences are largest, accounts for the overall difference in the proportions of whites and blacks who serve.

In order to measure the benefits or costs of military service, the prestige scores and wages 8 years after entry are regressed on a dummy variable indicating whether or not a man has been in the armed forces during his first 8 years in the labor force and four educational attainment dummy variables. In addition, the average prestige scores and wages in each of the race by education categories were calculated (see Table 5.9).

Whites with some military service in this period have jobs averaging 1.0 prestige points *below* those with no such service, holding educational attainment constant. Black veterans have jobs averaging 2.0 points *above* those of the men who do not serve. Neither effect is very large, the military service variable adds 1.0% to the variance explained by education for whites, 0.6% for blacks.[3] These summary statistics obscure the interaction between military service and education. Military service has a *positive* effect on the prestige scores of whites with some high school or with less education and a *negative* effect on men with some college and college graduates. For whites, veterans with no high school or some high school gain about one prestige point, there is no effect on high school graduates, men with some college lose about one point; and college

---

[3] These are estimates of the additional variances explained by adding five dummy variables to the regression of occupational prestige on education. They describe, *for each of the five levels of education separately*, whether or not a respondent has been in the armed forces.

TABLE 5.9 MEAN OCCUPATIONAL PRESTIGE AND WAGES EIGHT YEARS AFTER ENTRY, BY VETERAN STATUS' EDUCATION EIGHT YEARS AFTER ENTRY AND BY RACE

Race and Education Eight Years after Entry	Mean Occupational Prestige — Any Military Service?		Mean Wages ($/month) — Any Military Service?	
	No	Yes	No	Yes
White				
No high school	26.8	28.1	313	314
Some high school	31.9	32.9	389	374
High school graduate	36.0	36.1	492	424
Some college	41.5	40.7	537	477
College graduate	59.0	51.7	705	615
Total	38.1	37.7	479	447
Number of cases	330	518	289	413
Black				
No high school	22.2	23.6	254	283
Some high school	24.5	27.0	333	353
High school graduate	27.4	30.7	377	394
Some college	34.9	36.5	406	453
College graduate	52.5	44.7	493	564
Total	25.7	30.5	320	392
Number of cases	395	343	359	362

graduates who serve have prestige scores averaging 7.3 points below those of nonveterans.

A similar relationship is found for blacks, only the "break even" point moves up one level of education. Blacks in the four lowest educational attainment categories, up to and including some college, gain between 1.4 and 3.3 prestige points by serving. Among college graduates, black veterans average only 44.7 prestige points for the jobs held 8 years after entry, in comparison to the 52.5 point average for men with no such service, so the difference is as large as that found for whites.

No comparable interaction takes place when wages at the point 8 years after entry are substituted for prestige. At *every* level of education white veterans *lose* income, while blacks uniformly gain income from such service. The regressions show that military service, holding educational attainment constant, lowers white income by an average of $54 per month and raises black income by $26 per month. Holding education constant, military service explains an additional .7% of the variation in wages for whites, 4.8% for blacks. The income deficit suffered by white veterans increases steadily from zero for men with no high school to $80 per month for college graduates. Among blacks, the income *gains* of military service rise with increasing education, from $30 per month to $70 per month.

These results can be combined with our previous finding, that at the point 8 years after entry, white veterans have .22 more units of education, and black veterans .04 more units of education, than whites and blacks who have not served. This difference partly compensates for the white deficit found here; the net impact of military service is to leave white prestige scores unchanged and lower white wages by $39 per month, while black prestige scores are raised 2.1 points and black wages are raised $28 per month. The complexity of these results and their rather small magnitudes certainly show why there might be disagreements in the literature. The implication of our findings is that the overall impact of service in the armed forces makes a far less interesting object of research than does its impact on specific racial and educational groups.

MULTIVARIATE ANALYSIS OF THE JOB
HELD 8 YEARS AFTER ENTRY

So far we have examined the relationship of the respondent's prestige score and wages 8 years after entry to those of his earlier jobs and to education. This section presents a regression analysis of the quality of the later jobs similar to the ones performed earlier for the first job and for the job held two years after entry. This time the independent variables describe not only the individual's family background, jobs before entry, education, marital status, and the method of finding the job held after 8 years, and its industry; but also his first job after entry. The objective is to discover if some other characteristics of his first job, besides its prestige score and wages, might influence later occupational achievement. For example, we have found that men who moved between entry and the start of their first jobs do get higher first job wages as a result, these regressions will measure whether or not such earlier moves had any long term effects on prestige scores and wages. The prestige regressions are in Table 5.10, the wage regressions in Table 5.12, and the variance estimates in Table 5.11.

The Prestige Regression

As shown in Table 5.10, the total of thirty-two variables explains 47.8% of the variation in the occupational prestige score of whites 8 years after entry; for blacks the proportion is slightly lower, 43.9%. These values are somewhat greater than those obtained in the regression analysis of the first job prestige score, which amounted to 38.8% and 28.7% respectively; so, the level of uncertainty in the stratification process declines as the respondents acquire more work experience. The impact of family background, when these four variables alone are used as predictors, remains approximately constant over the 8 years, it accounts for 12.5% of the variance for whites, and 8.4% for blacks—the corresponding figures for the first job after entry are 9.0% and 10.5%. Blau and Duncan (1967:178) also find that the relationship between respondent's job and that of his father does not decline appreciably for their older age cohorts. Almost all of the effect of family background is mediated through the long chain of events connecting it to later jobs. Its small *direct* effects have conflicting directions—whites whose mothers have more education and whose fathers have *less* education have higher prestige scores 8 years after entry. A much larger sample might enable us to make something of these results, but the main finding is certainly that the principle effects of family background are mediated by intervening variables, such as those describing education and first job.

The respondent's educational attainment exerts the single most powerful influence on his later prestige score, as measured by either the zero-order or unique variance (see Table 5.11). When added to family background, education increases the explained variance by 24.5% for whites and 22.1% for blacks. The relative positions of the five major

TABLE 5.10   REGRESSION OF OCCUPATIONAL PRESTIGE EIGHT YEARS AFTER
ENTRY ON FAMILY BACKGROUND, EDUCATION EIGHT YEARS
AFTER ENTRY, NUMBER OF JOBS BEFORE ENTRY, FIRST JOB,
AND CHARACTERISTICS OF THE JOB HELD EIGHT YEARS AFTER
ENTRY, BY RACE

Independent Variable	Regression Coefficient		Standardized Regression Coefficient	
	White	Black	White	Black
Family background				
Father's education	-.49	.63	-.070†	.094†
Mother's education	.75	-.23	.090*	-.031
Father's occupation	-.042	-.002	-.037	-.002
Number of siblings	-.01	.19	-.003	.069†
Education eight years after entry				
Some high school	2.9	1.5	.075†	.062
High school graduate	5.5	3.5	.197*	.151*
Some college	9.5	8.6	.220*	.214*
College graduate	17.8	17.8	.467*	.333*
Number of jobs before entry				
Full-time	.18	.37	.042	.043
Part-time	.32	-.69	.028	-.068†
First job				
Occupational prestige	.27	.26	.234*	.215*
Starting wages	-.0055	-.0049	-.054	-.054
Geographic move	-2.8	.1	-.062	.043
Distance of move	.0044	-.001	.062	-.019
Marital Status	2.2	1.8	.036	.032
Method of locating job				
Direct	-1.0	.8	-.036	.037
Promotion	-6.7	-7.8	-.047	-.052
Industry				
Military service	-.4	.0	-.010	-.001
Manufacturing	.3	0.2	.009	.008
Transportation	-.3	-1.3	-.006	-.018
Trade	2.0	1.3	.054	.044
Finance & public admin.	-5.5	1.0	-.060†	.014
Service	-2.1	-1.0	-.044	-.028
Job held eight years after entry				
Military service	-.8	.6	-.027	.026
Marital status	1.9	-.4	.064†	-.020
Method of locating job				
Direct	3.0	.4	.108*	.021
Promotion	5.8	5.6	.157*	.134*
Industry				
Manufacturing	0.6	3.1	.018	.128*
Transportation	1.2	0.6	.025	.015
Trade	-3.1	2.6	-.079†	.088†
Finance & public admin.	3.8	7.8	.101*	.271*
Service	6.6	8.2	.152*	.251*
Regression constant	17.5	13.2		

* Statistically significant at .01
† Statistically significant at .05

TABLE 5.11 PROPORTION OF VARIANCE IN OCCUPATIONAL, PRESTIGE AND WAGES EIGHT YEARS AFTER ENTRY EXPLAINED BY FIVE GROUPS OF VARIABLES, BY RACE

Percent of Variance Explained

Dependent Variable and Group of Independent Variables	White				Black			
	Zero-Order	Unique	Addi-tional	Cumu-lative	Zero-Order	Unique	Addi-tional	Cumu-lative
Occupational prestige eight years after entry								
Family background	12.5	0.5	12.5	12.5	8.4	0.7	8.4	8.4
Education eight years after entry	36.2	6.5	24.5	37.0	28.8	8.2	22.1	30.5
Number of jobs before entry	15.4	0.2	0.5	37.5	2.0	0.4	0.3	30.8
First job	25.9	4.5	5.0	42.5	21.6	4.3	5.3	36.1
Job held eight years after entry	21.4	5.3	5.3	47.8	22.2	7.8	7.8	43.9
Wages eight years after entry								
Family background	5.2	0.2	5.2	5.2	7.8	1.0	7.8	7.8
Education eight years after entry	14.9	0.7	9.9	15.1	17.0	2.4	10.9	18.7
Number of jobs before entry	13.6	0.9	3.2	18.3	1.5	0.0	0.1	18.7
First job	26.1	10.7	10.9	29.2	29.2	14.8	15.3	34.0
Job held eight years after entry	6.8	2.4	2.4	31.6	10.2	3.4	3.4	37.4

categories of education are quite similar for the two races. White high school graduates have jobs averaging 5.5 points above the lowest group, those with no high school, compared to 3.5 points for blacks. For both races, 17.8 prestige points separate college graduates from the lowest group. So, again, there is a weak tendency for the blacks in the middle level of education to gain slightly less from their schooling than the corresponding whites. We should note that since some changes in educational attainment occur after the first job, our placement of education at this early point in the temporal ordering of the groups of variables seems open to question. However, the fact that the *changes* in educational attainment between entry and the point 8 years later have been found to be quite unrelated to the other variables in this regression means that use of a single set of education variables does not exaggerate the effect of education—it appears that about one-tenth of the impact of education, 3.3% for whites and 1.2% for blacks, can be attributed to changes after entry, the larger white variance being the result of higher levels of educational mobility among white respondents.[4]

The impact of jobs held before entry on prestige 8 years after entry is very much the same as on prestige of first job (see Table 5.12). The two

[4] An attempt was made to introduce the effect of education as two sets of dummy variables, one for the respondent's attainment at entry and one to measure it's value 8 years after entry. Unfortunately, the number of individuals making transitions was not large enough to produce a reliable estimate of the effect of the latter, and the high correlations among some of the variables in the two sets produced very large errors in the estimates for both sets of regression coefficients. However, by using a substitution procedure, it was possible to arrive at a variance estimate for the impact of educational changes after entry. The resulting stepwise additions to the variance explained are as follows (these are modifications of the third and seventh columns in Table 5.11):

	Whites	Blacks
Family background	12.5%	8.4%
Education at entry	22.1	20.2
Pre-entry jobs	0.5	0.4
First job	4.1	5.9
Change in education	3.3	1.2
Later job	5.3	7.8
Total	47.8%	43.9%

variables measuring the number of full-time and of part-time jobs before entry have a comparatively large zero-order effect on prestige for whites, but almost none for blacks. With all the other variables held constant, numbers of early jobs have very small direct effects for both races. The two variables increase the variance explained by family background and education by only .5% for whites and .3% for blacks. So pre-entry jobs do play a significant intervening role in the white stratification process, primarily linking educational attainment with later occupation variables; for blacks their role is of no importance.

The first job after entry has quite a large effect on the job held 8 years later, though much of this effect can be traced back to family background and education. The zero-order variances attributable to this set of thirteen variables amount to 25.9% for whites and 21.6% for blacks—but the increases produced when the temporally earlier variables are held constant amount to only 5.0% for whites and 5.3% for blacks. Of the thirteen variables, only the occupational prestige score of the first job has a long-term effect of any importance—for both races, approximately one-quarter of its value is added into the estimate of the prestige score after 8 years.

There are a number of statistically insignificant but interesting effects of the first job. For example, men whose first jobs are located by direct methods have prestige scores, 8 years later, that are 1.0 points below those who found their first jobs with the help of friends or family. But, our earlier analysis shows that they had *first jobs* with prestige scores 2.3 points *above* the other group—and the two effects partially balance one another out. Industry of first job, respondent's marital status, and moves all have similar small effects. It is important to comment on one of the insignificant results: Wages of first job, with all the other variables held constant, exerts a small *negative* effect on prestige after 8 years, of about equal magnitude for each race. The suggestion, though the effect is not a large one, is that individuals who maximize prestige, may do so at some cost in terms of wages. The important implication of our finding that first job prestige is sufficient to capture almost all of the long-term effect of the first job is that models that attempt to describe this process in terms of occupational prestige can use this one variable to measure the effect of the first job.

The final set of variables in Table 5.12 describe the industry of the job held 8 years after entry,[5] how it is located, the respondent's marital status and whether or not he served in the armed forces during the 8 years after entry. They uniquely explain 5.3% of the variation in the prestige scores for whites, 7.8% for blacks—again the values are very much smaller than the corresponding zero-order effects. As in the case of the first job after entry, men who locate their own jobs and do not rely on their friends or families obtain better jobs, by 3.0 prestige points for whites and .4 points for blacks; the differences are still larger, 5.8 and 5.6 points for whites and blacks respectively, for the men who are promoted into the jobs they hold 8 years after entry. Several of the dummy variables measuring the industry of the job have significant effects—for both races, jobs in primary industry and construction, and in transportation rank lowest and those in finance and public administration and service highest. White jobs in wholesale and retail trade are very low but are in the middle of the distribution for whites; also blacks' jobs in manufacturing rank higher for blacks than for whites. These differences are a reflection of

[5] In the 8 years after entry there was considerable change in the distribution of workers within industries. The following table shows the results:

	First job after entry		Eight years after entry	
	White	Black	White	Black
Military service (percent	17	17	7	9
Civilian industry (percent)				
Primary and construction	32	34	21	19
Manufacturing	27	26	32	32
Transportation	8	3	10	8
Trade	19	20	16	18
Finance and public administration	3	3	9	9
Service	11	14	12	14
Total (civilian)	100	100	100	100
Number of cases			850	738

For the first job, approximately one-half of the workers in the "primary and construction" category are in agriculture, for both races; 8 years after entry, about one-third of the men in this category are in agriculture. In the regression, the men in the armed forces at the point 8 years after entry are placed in the "finance and public administration" category, since they are public employees. For these individuals, no wages are defined.

TABLE 5.12   REGRESSION OF WAGES EIGHT YEARS AFTER ENTRY ON
FAMILY BACKGROUND, EDUCATION EIGHT YEARS AFTER
ENTRY, NUMBER OF JOBS BEFORE ENTRY, FIRST JOB,
AND CHARACTERISTICS OF THE JOB HELD EIGHT YEARS
AFTER ENTRY, BY RACE

Independent Variable	Regression Coefficient		Standardized Regression Coefficient	
	White	Black	White	Black
Family background				
Father's education	6.6	-5.0	.042	-.049
Mother's education	-5.9	10.4	-.037	.094†
Father's occupation	-.49	.62	-.023	.044
Number of siblings	1.0	-2.5	-.011	-.060
Education eight years after entry				
Some high school	-9	27	-.013	.076
High school	19	41	.037	.115†
Some college	43	72	.053	.117*
College graduate	91	156	.127	.191*
Number of jobs before entry				
Full-time	11.7	.3	.098†	.002
Part-time	6.1	-1.5	.043	-.010
First job				
Occupational prestige	3.08	-.68	.142*	-.036
Starting wages	.541	.561	.283*	.406*
Geographic move	60	43	.067	.079
Distance of move	-.160	-.090	-.12*	-.086
Marital Status	114	-19	.097†	-.022
Method of locating job				
Direct	-9	27	-.017	.078†
Promotion	-64	-51	-.024	-.022
Industry				
Military service	-1	64	-.001	.142*
Manufacturing	-18	-13	-.029	-.032
Transportation	-80	6	-.075	-.006
Trade	21	6	.030	.014
Finance & public admin.	-72	-48	-.042	-.042
Service	77	21	.086*	.040
Job held eight years after entry				
Military service	-15	7	-.028	.020
Marital status	32	17	.056	.050
Method of locating job				
Direct	36	1	.069*	.004
Promotion	78	79	.113†	.121*
Industry				
Manufacturing	-53	30	-.094†	.081
Transportation	-13	8	-.014	.012
Trade	-77	-20	-.105*	-.044
Finance & public admin.	-35	9	-.048	.019
Service	-96	-37	-.118*	-.074
Regression constant	215	160		

* Statistically significant at .01
† Statistically significant at .05

the gross categorization used, since the range of occupations within each industry is very large. The married white respondents have slightly better jobs than the unmarried, for blacks there is a positive but insignificant effect in the same direction.

The regression allows us to make a final estimate of the impact of military service, with all the other variables held constant. White veterans have jobs averaging .8 prestige points lower than nonveterans. About one-third of the men who served took first jobs in the armed forces, so the average difference is increased by one-third of the difference between the military group and the average score of the six civilian industrial categories, which amounts to about −.3 points. We estimate, then, that white veterans have jobs which average 1.1 prestige points below nonveterans with the same characteristics. A similar procedure places black veterans .7 prestige points ahead of those who do not serve. These results are both of negligible magnitude.

The regression results for blacks and whites do not differ in any important respect. The differences that are found have very little impact on the outcome of the stratification process. A good example is our finding that pre-entry jobs play a role in transmitting the impact of education to prestige of later jobs for whites, but not for blacks. However, the net impact of these jobs on later prestige scores is very small. In addition, the greater predictability of white prestige scores remains, but the difference is only one-half as large as that for the first job after entry.

The Wage Regression

The entire group of variables explains 31.6% of the variation in respondent's wages 8 years after entry for whites, 37.4% for blacks. The corresponding variances for the starting wage of the first job are 28.1% and 15.3%. So, while the prestige stratification process is a more uncertain one for blacks, this is not the case for the wage dimension. A similar change occurs in the impact of family background. For the first job, it explains 11.5% of the variation in wages for whites, but only 3.8% for blacks; 8 years after entry the variances are 5.2% for whites and 7.8% for blacks. Of course, almost all of its impact flows through other variables. The one statistically significant direct effect is that of mother's education, which raises blacks' wages by $10.4 per month for each unit on the 10-point scale.

Educational attainment has a much weaker influence on wages than on prestige scores. The unique effect of the four dummy variables is only 0.7% of the variance for whites, 2.4% for blacks—their stepwise contribution amounts to 9.9% for whites, 10.9% for blacks.[6] These values are less than one-half as large as those obtained in the prestige regression above. The range of the four dummy variables is significantly greater for blacks, $72 per month separates black high school graduates from those with no high school, and $84 per month separates college graduates from high school graduates. The corresponding values for whites are about one-third smaller.

As in the prestige analysis, jobs held before entry have a much stronger effect on white wages—each full-time job is worth an average of $11.7 and each part-time job $6.1 per month. For blacks their impact is negligible.

Using the stepwise procedure, the group of thirteen variables describing the first job after entry is the most important single influence on wages 8 years after entry, accounting for 10.9% of the variance for whites and 15.3% for blacks—so it exerts two to three times more impact on wages than on prestige scores. The starting wage of the first job is by far the most important of these variables, about one-half of its value is added into the

[6] The application of the stepwise variance procedure generates the following modified estimates, which include both education at entry and educational gains made in the 8 years after entry:

	Whites	Blacks
Family background	5.2%	7.8%
Education at entry	15.6	11.1
Pre-entry jobs	1.5	.0
First job	8.4	15.3
Change in education	−1.5	−.2
Later job	2.4	3.4
Total	31.6%	37.4%

The negative estimates for the change in education show that a respondent's education 8 years after entry is a *poorer* predictor of his wages 8 years after entry than is his education at entry, with all the other variables held constant. Men who acquire more education *cannot* be assured of wage gains as a result. There is weak evidence to show that for some of the intermediate levels of education the net effects of educational gains are negative.

estimate of the later wage value. For whites, the occupational prestige score of the first job also exerts a considerable positive effect on later wages, while for blacks there is an insignificant, but negative effect. Hence, the two dimensions of job quality operate more independently for blacks. A number of the other variables have statistically significant effects on wages. In particular, blacks with first jobs in the armed forces and those who locate their jobs using direct methods have higher wages, as do whites who are married, who are in the service industry, and who do not move. These results are not readily interpretable, and many of the variables are highly correlated with the starting wages of the first job.

The last group of variables, describing the respondent's marital status 8 years after entry, the industry of his job, and how it is located, and whether or not he served in the armed forces, explains only 2.4% of the variance in wages for whites and 3.4% for blacks—about one-half of its effect on the prestige scores. The industry variables have a much stronger effect for whites, while men of both races who obtain these jobs by promotion are better paid, in each case by $78 per month. Married men appear to have slightly higher incomes, too. Using the procedure employed for prestige, a calculation of the effect of military service finds white veterans earning $14 per month *below* nonveterans, and black veterans earning $28 per month *above* nonveterans—of course, this disregards the earnings losses veterans accumulate during the terms of military service.

This analysis shows clearly that there are racial differences in the relationships of wages to the five groups of contributing factors described here and that the relative impact of these factors is not the same as is found for the prestige variable. Wage levels are more determined by past work experience—the first job does much more to set a pattern for later wages than it does for occupational prestige, which remains quite tightly tied to educational attainment. Taking the two elements of conventional stratification models, family background and educational attainment, it is possible to explain 37.0% of the variation in occupational prestige scores for whites, but less than one-half that much, 15.1% of the variance, in white wage values at that point. The difference is not so great for blacks, 30.5% versus 18.7%. The level of the first job is between two and three times more important a determinant of wages than of prestige scores. The clear implication is that somewhat different strategies will be necessary to develop wage, income, and perhaps wealth stratification models to accompany or be integrated with the models that now use socioeconomic or prestige rankings of occupations as the major variables.

Allocating the Racial Difference

Once more using Duncan's procedure, we can examine the contribution of each of six groups of variables to the net difference between the mean prestige scores and mean wages of blacks and whites. The allocation of the 8.6 point prestige difference is as follows: family background 3.3 points, education at entry .3 points, pre-entry jobs .5 points, first job .3 points, change in education after entry .4 points, characteristics of the job held 8 years after entry .0 points. The largest single effect is the residual attributable to discrimination (or unmeasured variables), which amounts to 3.8 prestige points. Over 80% of the gap between the races is due to the combination of differences in family background and the "pure" effect of discrimination.

The result is no different for wages. In this case the $110 per month gap is allocated in the following way: family background $40, education at entry $7, pre-entry jobs $8, first job $2, change in education after entry $5, characteristics of the job held eight years after entry $9, unexplained residual $39 per month. Again, family background and "pure" discrimination account for the greatest part of the difference, though there is a small accumulation of additional deficits at each point in the career. In both cases, a considerable part of the gap between the races cannot be assigned to measurable differences, such as those in family background, education, and so on. It is unlikely that the addition of further factors describing individual careers more closely will lower the residual appreciably. The similarity of the wage and prestige results, once education is held constant, is quite remarkable—even though the two variables are not strongly related to one another.

Factors Affecting Mobility

In Tables 5.13 and 5.14 the prestige scores and wages of the job 8 years after entry are regressed on the most important variables describing our respondents' careers. The problem we wish to address is the identification of the factors responsible for mobility in these two occupational dimensions. Rather than creating a mobility variable that measures the change in prestige or wages, we can examine the variables that predict their values at the point 8 years after entry, when the levels of the first job and of the job held 2 years after entry are held constant. This makes it possible

TABLE 5.13   REGRESSION OF OCCUPATIONAL PRESTIGE EIGHT YEARS AFTER ENTRY ON FAMILY BACKGROUND, EDUCATION AT ENTRY, NUMBER OF JOBS BEFORE ENTRY, LEVEL OF FIRST JOB, LEVEL OF JOB HELD TWO YEARS AFTER ENTRY, MILITARY SERVICE, AND EDUCATION EIGHT YEARS AFTER ENTRY, BY RACE

Independent Variable	Regression Coefficient		Standardized Regression Coefficient		Correlation with Dependent Variable	
	White	Black	White	Black	White	Black
Family background						
Father's education	-.40	.59	-.056	.089†	.257	.274
Mother's education	.56	-.09	.067†	-.013	.294	.236
Father's occupation	.044	-.012	.039	-.013	-.194	-.131
Number of siblings	.09	-.013	.020	-.005	.274	.188
Education at entry	.53	1.19	.067	.171	.583	.481
Number of jobs before entry						
Full-time	.26	.46	.040	.054	.363	.141
Part-time	.16	-.53	.021	-.056	.280	.063
First job						
Prestige	.093	.193	.081†	.155*	.462	.411
Wages	-.0023	-.0059	-.022	-.066	.250	.129
Job held two years after entry						
Prestige	.323	.193	.267*	.155*	.544	.452
Wages	-.0023	-.0006	-.031	-.008	.242	.185
Military service	.4	.8	.014	.038	-.015	.218
Education eight years after entry	2.45	1.26	.334*	.186	.592	.491
Regression constant	9.8*	10.8*				
Percent of variance explained by all variables	43.8	32.7				

*   Statistically significant at .01
†   Statistically significant at .05

to avoid the effects of regression toward the mean commonly found in this mobility analysis—for the men who make the greatest gains will be those who started out in the worst positions, since they literally "have nowhere to go but up."

    Taking the prestige variable first, we find that the prestige score of the first job and the one 2 years after entry explain 31.3% of the variance

TABLE 5.14   REGRESSION OF WAGES EIGHT YEARS AFTER ENTRY ON FAMILY BACKGROUND, EDUCATION AT ENTRY, NUMBER OF JOBS BEFORE ENTRY, LEVEL OF FIRST JOB, LEVEL OF JOB HELD TWO YEARS AFTER ENTRY, MILITARY SERVICE, AND EDUCATION EIGHT YEARS AFTER ENTRY, BY RACE

Independent Variable	Regression Coefficient		Standardized Regression Coefficient		Correlation with Dependent Variable	
	White	Black	White	Black	White	Black
Family background						
Father's education	7.9	-1.0	.059†	-.010	.179	.202
Mother's education	-3.8	8.4	-.024	.076	.184	.255
Father's occupation	-.6	.3	-.026	.019	-.142	-.077
Number of siblings	5.3	.7	.058†	.017	.158	.128
Education at entry	43.0	-15.7	.293*	-.148	.481	.409
Number of jobs before entry						
Full-time	.6	3.1	.005	.023	.341	.109
Part-time	-.4	-2.7	-.002	-.019	.264	.095
First job						
Prestige	3.04	-.15	.140*	-.008	.336	.194
Wages	-.606	.238	-.317*	.172*	.405	.474
Job held two years after entry						
Prestige	-2.19	-.54	-.096†	-.028	.342	.227
Wages	1.181	.389	.859*	.323*	.724	.528
Military service	9	33	.018	.097*	-.061	.216
Education eight years after entry	-4.3	33.9	-.031	.324*	.422	.396
Regression constant	76	120				
Percent of variance explained by all variables	63.0	35.2				

* Statistically significant at .01
† Statistically significant at .05

in prestige scores after 8 years in the labor force for whites, 21.6% for blacks. The addition of all the other variables increases these values to 43.8% and 32.7%, respectively. So, about one-sixth of the remaining unexplained variance is accounted for by the twelve additional independent variables. We noted in the examination of the changes within categories of education in Table 5.4 that the men in the higher categories of education are the ones who make the greatest prestige gains over the 8 years. In this regression, except for earlier prestige scores, we find that the most important variables are those measuring education, and that their signs are positive. So, men with more education experience more prestige mobility.[7] There are two other small effects that reach statistical significance—whites with higher levels of mother's education and blacks with higher values of father's education have more mobility. An interesting, but statistically insignificant, effect is exerted by the wage values—men with higher starting wages at their first job or at the point 2 years after entry have *lower* prestige scores 8 years after entry (this effect is also found in the larger regression in Table 5.10).

The starting wages of the first job and the wage values at the point 2 years after entry together account for 55.2% of the variation in white wages 8 years after entry, 29.0% in the case of blacks. When the other variables are inserted in the regression, these values rise to 63.0% and 35.2%, respectively. Hence they reduce the unexplained variance by about one-sixth for whites and by about one-tenth for blacks. Once more educational attainment has the largest effect. Men with more education experience more wage mobility. In this case, there are a number of small statistically significant effects for whites—men whose fathers have more education, who have more siblings, and who have higher first job prestige scores and lower prestige scores 2 years after entry are all upwardly mobile, as are blacks who serve in the armed forces.

As was found in the similar educational attainment regression, it is much easier to predict the level of the outcome than to predict mobility, though in this case we are a good deal more successful. For both the prestige and the wage variables it is found that the single most important predictor of upward mobility is education; family background, pre-entry jobs, military service, and the other occupational dimension (i.e., prestige as a predictor of wage mobility, and vice versa) have very little effect.

---

[7] For whites, it is found that respondent's education at the point 8 years after entry has a large effect on the prestige score, but that education at entry is relatively unimportant; for blacks, the two education measures are about equally powerful. The difference results from the fact that whites experience more educational mobility, so their two education variables are more dissimilar. The regression routine heavily weights the variable with the stronger relationship to the prestige score 8 years after entry. As we have noted, there are insufficient cases to properly separate out these two very highly intercorrelated effects, so we do not venture an interpretation of these patterns. It may be that the extent of educational *mobility* is a useful predictor of later prestige scores.

PATH ANALYSIS TO THE POINT 8 YEARS AFTER ENTRY

Our consideration of the middle-term impact of entry closes with a discussion of path models that include twelve key variables describing the stratification process up to the point 8 years after entry (see Figure 5.1). In part, it will serve to recapitulate the findings of the above analysis. Since the wages of jobs in the armed forces are not defined and because the path analysis includes all men, it has been necessary to assume that the relationships between wage rates of civilians and the other variables hold for the sample as a whole—the "pairwise present" regression routine automatically makes such an assumption. The paths were established using a true stepwise regression procedure, that is, *forward* selection of new variables with significant additional effects at .05, *with the deletion of previously included variables* that fall below statistical significance, again at .05. Some other procedure might have resulted in a slightly different model. Any such selection algorithm depends on the researcher making some very strong assumptions about the theoretical structure of the process being analyzed. The common method of attempting first to delete paths that span the greatest distance in time makes assumptions that tend to direct as much of the effect of earlier variables through intervening variables as is possible. The correlation matrices in Appendix C allow the interested reader to try his or her own hand at a path analysis, employing whatever variables and selection procedure might be desired.

It was decided to include prestige and wage measures for the first job and for the points 2 and 8 years after entry. We judged that the inclusion of these values at the point 1 year after entry would so clutter the diagram as to make it unintelligible. Again the prestige and wage values at the same point in time are connected through correlations of their residuals.[8] The

---

[8] Should direct effects of occupational prestige on wages *at the same point in time* be permitted, the following modifications to the path model take place:

Path to	From	Whites	Blacks
Wages of first job	Mother's education	.142	—
	Number of siblings	−.073	—
	Education at entry	.238	.315
	Prestige of first job	.144	.102
	Residual	.896	.931

commentary here focuses on the jobs held after entry, since the earlier parts of the process have been discussed above. The spatial arrangements of the variables in the diagrams for blacks and whites are somewhat different, their positions have been shifted to improve the clarity of the diagrams. Simplified path diagrams, with eight major variables, are in Figure 5.2.

The path models show up the difference between the wage and prestige dimensions of the stratification process. More paths converge on the wage variables, and they are more tightly tied to previous wage values and less strongly to education than is the case for prestige. Wage values at one point in time exert very strong effects on later wages, and for whites the prestige scores directly affect both later prestige values and later wages. For both races, the variables defined for the first job and at the point 2 years after entry directly influence the job 8 years after entry. It is clear that once education at entry is defined, the direct and indirect effects of education, prestige, and wages dominate the small effects of family background. The mobility rates within the prestige and wage dimensions are more closely connected for whites than for blacks. Some of the path coefficients in the white model are negative. Featherman (1971:301) also

Path to	From	White	Black
Wages two years after entry	Father's education	−.079	−.074
	Mother's education	—	.104
	Education at entry	.119	.189
	Prestige of first job	−.086	—
	Starting wages of first job	.668	.700
	Prestige two years after entry	.151	—
	Residual	.674	.602
Wages 8 years after entry	Mother's education	—	.071
	Number of siblings	.059	—
	Education at entry	.222	—
	Prestige of first job	.125	—
	Starting wages of first job	−.318	.174
	Prestige two years after entry	−.140	—
	Wages two years after entry	.858	.297
	Education eight years after entry	—	.167
	Prestige eight years after entry	.145	.091
	Residual	.600	.807

Note the consistently stronger effects of prestige on wages for whites.

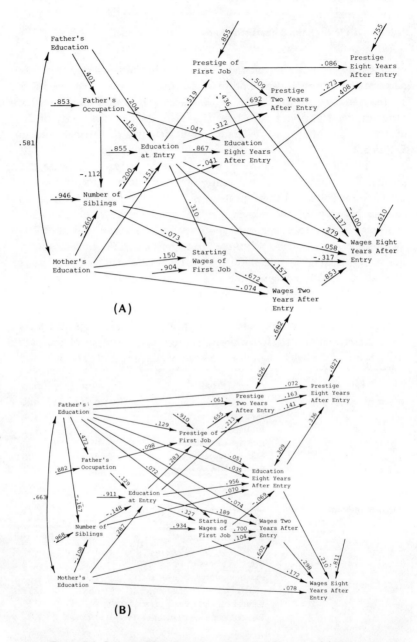

Figure 5.1. Path model to the point eight years after entry (a) Whites. Correlations of residuals of prestige and wages: first job after entry = .145, two years after entry = .067, eight years after entry = .154. (b) Blacks. Correlations of residuals of prestige and wages: first job after entry = .099, two years after entry = .074, eight years after entry = .071.

166

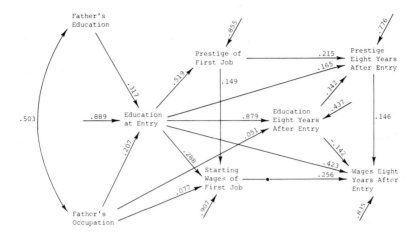

(A)

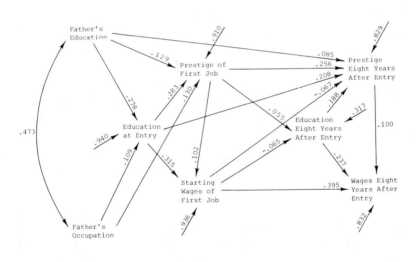

(B)

Figure 5.2. Simplified path model to the point eight years after entry (a) whites and (b) blacks.

finds some such effects. The implication is that later occupational attainment may depend not only on earlier occupation levels, but also on the extent of earlier occupational mobility—since the negative effects can always be transformed into positive effects of mobility measures.

There are also important racial differences in the roles played by background variables. The family background variables, particularly father's education, exert a stronger influence on the process for blacks. For blacks, father's education directly affects all three of the prestige variables, the starting wages of the first job, the wages of the job 2 years after entry, and educational attainment at entry and 8 years after entry; mother's education, father's occupation, and the number of siblings all have some small direct effects on later achievement, but their indirect effects, transmitted through education at entry, are more systematic and stronger.

One curious result is that, for whites, the respondent's education at entry, rather than at the point 8 years after entry, directly affects the value of his wages 8 years after entry. This is not an artifact of the forward selection procedure, backward elimination would have achieved the same result. Thus the educational level at which a white worker starts out is clearly of more importance in determining wages than whatever he does later to improve it. Again the conclusion must be that the level of entry plays a far more important role for wages than for prestige values. No such result is obtained for blacks, presumably because of their lower levels of educational mobility, though, as the regression in the previous section showed, education 8 years after entry is a slightly poorer predictor of black wages 8 years after entry than is education at entry.

SUMMARY

In the 8 years after entry into the labor force, the differences among men with various levels of educational attainment and between whites and blacks increase markedly. What is most interesting about the changes in job quality is that at the lowest levels of education, where there is little racial difference in their respective prestige scores and starting wages for the first job, whites are substantially better off than blacks after 8 years. Though black college graduates have significantly poorer jobs than their white counterparts, a pattern observed in examining the first job after entry, they get no further behind during this 8-year period. About one-third of the gap between blacks and whites, in prestige scores and wages, is due to differences in their family background; another one-third is attributable to the combination of education, quality of first job, pre-entry jobs, and a group of variables describing the job held 8 years after entry; and the "pure" effect of discrimination—the difference that could not be accounted for by all these factors—is responsible for the last one-third.

The patterns of job mobility found in the first 2 years after entry and in the examination of the duration of the first job do not change in the next 6 years. Men with more education change jobs more frequently, and whites experience more mobility than blacks. Higher rates of job mobility have little impact on the quality of the job a man finally holds—except that men who continue to work at their first jobs have slightly lower wages.

Significant educational mobility takes place in the 8 years after entry. Approximately one-quarter of the whites and one-tenth of the blacks gain some education in this period, the result of which is to increase the gap between white and black levels of education. Just over one-half of the educational gains observed result in the respondent moving between two adjacent categories in the five category classification. For both races it proved impossible to predict accurately which individuals would make these gains. The conventional stratification variables, such as family background and level of first job, do not explain more than a fraction of the educational mobility that occurs.

More than 60% of the white respondents and just under one-half of the blacks serve in the armed forces sometime during the 8 years after entry. The overall impact of this military service on later prestige scores and wages is relatively weak, but a number of interesting patterns arise. First it is found that veterans make somewhat larger educational gains in the 8 years after entry, and they generally have higher prestige scores than nonveterans of the same race and level of education—except for college graduates of both races and for whites with some college. The veterans with higher levels of education have poorer jobs than their nonveteran counterparts. At every level of education, white veterans have lower wages and black veterans higher wages, at the point 8 years after entry, than do their nonveteran counterparts. When many variables are held constant in large regressions, it is clear that the net effects of military service are very small, except that black veterans have appreciably higher wages than men with the same characteristics who have not served.

A very large number of variables were combined in a regression analysis of the prestige scores and wages of respondents after 8 years in the labor force. Many individual findings emerged, but two more fundamental patterns showed themselves. First, it is clear that the wage and prestige dimensions of occupations are governed by different combinations of factors; The wage variables are more strongly affected by the wages and other characteristics of early jobs, while occupational prestige continues to bear a strong relationship to the respondent's education and to his family background. Second, while the prestige allocation processes for whites and blacks are very similar, there are a number of important differences in the relative strengths of the competing influences on white and black wage values. However, as has become clear, the *levels* of their jobs are quite different, in both prestige and wage terms. Also, the path analysis shows that the autonomy of the two dimensions of job quality is greater for blacks than for whites.

Conclusions 6

The objectives of this study have been to trace the careers of young American men as they enter the labor force, to discover the relative importance of a number of factors that govern the quality of the jobs held in this period and the roles they play in the stratification process, and to assess the impact of the mode and level of entry on the course of occupational careers as a whole. Each chapter has concluded with a summary, and our purpose here is to draw these findings together into a number of generalizations about entry into the labor force and the American social structure. To aid in this synthesis, some additional data are given in two tables summarizing the racial and educational differences during the whole of the time covered by the study.

SETTLING DOWN TO WORK

Though entry into the labor force has often been pictured as a particularly trying and uncertain time in a person's career, in the aggregate, the levels of jobs held and mobility do conform to "sensible" patterns. Most men find jobs very soon after they enter the labor force and hold only one or two jobs in the first 2 years after entry; a good part of the mobility that takes place involves men joining the armed forces after taking first jobs as civilians. Though the 2 years after entry are marked by relatively small shifts in the respondents' *average* prestige scores and wages, the increase in their values is distributed very unequally: Men with more education experience more upward mobility, especially in the prestige dimension;

and whites make twice the gains of blacks. Some meaningful changes in the relationships between variables also take place; for example, the correlation between educational attainment and the occupational prestige score of a respondent's job increases in the period after entry. But the basic patterns do not change.

It has also been possible to discover a logic to the occupational mobility taking place in the 2 years after entry. Coupled with the general tendency for the quality of jobs to rise as men gain more experience and additional education, their jobs fall more into line with their expectations—or at least with our estimate of the jobs they "should" expect on the basis of their levels of educational attainment. A disproportionate amount of mobility takes place among individuals whose first jobs are significantly poorer, as measured by their prestige scores, than those of the average respondent with the same education. This process of settling down to work, and of "correcting errors" arising in the selection of the first job, takes place very rapidly. Within 1 year after entry this pattern of mobility is readily apparent.

The detailed analysis of the duration of the first job has provided a number of important, and apparently original, findings about the nature of job mobility. The decision to change jobs is very strongly governed by an economic calculus—a single variable measuring the increase in wages during the first job accounts for almost one-half of the variance in first job duration. The level of wages at the *start* of the job and its prestige score have little impact on the decision to change jobs. Nor does the level of education of the respondent. The only personal characterstic that affects duration to any appreciable extent is marital status—married men display considerably less mobility. It is apparent that the individual decision to leave a particular job is largely a response to an evaluation of that job. Only to a very slight extent can some individuals be characterized as more likely to change jobs than others, the correlation between the duration of consecutive jobs held by the same respondent is very small, though not zero. The fact that job prestige scores play such an unimportant role in the mobility process suggests that mobility in this dimension, for an individual with a given level of education, is very difficult. But it certainly is possible to get better pay for doing a similar job for another firm. Of course, it may be that some variables describing the working conditions within a specific firm also play a role in mobility decisions.

OCCUPATIONAL DIFFERENCES
BETWEEN BLACKS AND WHITES

At almost every point in this analysis we have found evidence that the process of entry into the labor force works to the disadvantage of black Americans. We must emphasize the *continuous* nature of this process; the impact of racism does not descend at any one distinct point, instead the continuing accumulation of small deficits causes blacks to fall further and further behind whites. This should come as no surprise. A study such as this one, based on a relatively small number of cases, can add very little to the more accurate statistics describing the nature of these differences that can be found in the Census and in the monthly labor force surveys of the Bureau of Labor Statistics. What it can do is to add a processual dimension to the static measures of racial differences which are well known.

Table 6.1 provides a summary of the development of racial inequality, it presents the differences between the mean values for whites and blacks of the most important stratification variables, measured in units of standard deviations. Thus the first figure shows that the difference between the educational attainment of the average white respondent and the average black is equal to .38 standard deviations of the white value (.46, using the black standard deviation). Since the standard deviations of *each* of the variables is greater for whites, the differences are smaller when measured in white standard deviations—but the *pattern* of differences does not change. These standardized values make it possible to examine the racial differences, while eliminating the effects of the constantly shifting means, and to obtain a direct comparison of variables measured in the very different units of educational attainment, occupational prestige, and wages.

The most obvious pattern in the table is that the gap between whites and blacks increases in the period after entry. The educational attainment of the average black respondent is .46 standard deviations lower than that of his white counterpart at entry, .55 units lower after 8 years in the labor force. The gap in occupational prestige scores rises from .38 standard deviations for the first job after entry, to .49 after 2 years, and to .72 at the 8-year point. The difference in wages averages .31 standard deviations for the first job and grows to .35 after 2 years and to .42 after 8 years in

6.1   MEAN RACIAL DIFFERENCE FOR IMPORTANT STRATIFICATION VARIABLES

	Racial Difference (white mean–black mean)	
Variable	In Units Of White Standard Deviations	In Units Of Black Standard Deviations
Family background		
Father's education	.38	.46
Mother's education	.38	.42
Father's occupation	-.59	.43
Number of siblings	.64	.67
Number of jobs before entry		
Full-time	.42	.73
Part-time	.36	.57
Education		
At entry	.46	.52
Eight years after entry	.5.5	.62
Occupational pestige		
First job	.38	.51
One year after entry	.42	.57
Two years after entry	.49	.65
Eight years after entry	.72	.92
Wages		
First job	.31	.35
One year after entry	.32	.37
Two years after entry	.35	.48
Eight years after entry	.42	.66

the labor force. The increasing difference, in all three dimensions, graphically demonstrates the barriers faced by black workers.

In fact, these racial differences are larger than those that existed between the parents of these men. The mean values of father's education differ by .38 standard deviations, compared to a standard deviation of .55 for their sons after 8 years at work. Similarly, the racial difference in the father's occupational prestige score averages .64 standard deviations, compared to a difference of .72 standard deviations for their sons after 8 years in the labor force. While there is a temptation to conclude that the level of inequality has increased between the generations, we cannot do so, for the sample of fathers is not a random sample as is that of our respondents. The father with a larger family, and hence more sons, is more likely to appear in our survey than the man with a small family; and since fertility varies according to race and social class, we cannot easily estimate the true racial gap for the generation before that of these respondents.

The biggest difference between whites and blacks is in the occupational prestige scores. Especially at low levels of education, the wage differences are quite small. These differences arise from a number of causes, only some of which are dealt with here. Blacks are less likely to get promotion or on-the-job training than are whites. Though we have no data on the labor market itself, there is some evidence that its structure is such that blacks with low levels of education are able to locate jobs about as rapidly as whites with the same levels of education, but well-educated blacks find it far more difficult to locate jobs than their white counterparts.

While the racial differences are very systematic, race has far less impact on job quality than does educational attainment. The differences between blacks and whites with the same levels of education are small compared to those between high school graduates and college graduates of either race. Of course, race also figures in the differences in educational attainment levels. About one-half of the gap in the prestige and wage levels of whites and blacks is removed by equating educational differences.

Perhaps the most interesting finding bearing on the differences between whites and blacks is that relating to the development of these differences. The average gains, in wages and in occupational prestige, obtained in the transition from the first job after entry to the second, are almost identical for blacks and whites. However, what does vary is the duration of this first job. Blacks hold their first jobs an average of 1 year longer than whites, so the change in moving between the first and second jobs is spread out over a longer period for blacks. Thus the black *rate* of mobility is significantly lower. Similar findings emerge in other parts of the data—for example married men of both races tend to have longer job durations than single men, however this gap between the job durations of single and married men is twice as large for blacks as it if for whites. Similarly, a pay raise of a given size prolongs the job of a black worker by more than twice as long a period as it does for the corresponding white worker.

Once an individual has entered the labor force, by our definition, the likelihood of his gaining any additional education (at least in the next 8 years) is more than twice as great for whites as for blacks. Thus the point of entry marks a more important division between school and work for blacks. In a stratification system that has educational attainment as one of its most important components, the growth of the racial gap in education adds appreciably to the occupational deficits of blacks. Because of the stronger relationship between education and occupational prestige, and since wage values are more closely tied to earlier wages, the effect of the increased educational differential has much more of an impact on prestige values than on wages.

The beginnings of the careers of black respondents are marked by more uncertainty than is the case for whites. Family background explains 27.0% of the variation in education at entry for whites, 17.2% for blacks; using four groups of variables it is possible to account for 38.8% of the variance in whites first job prestige scores and 28.1% for blacks; for wages at entry the corresponding proportions are 28.7% and 15.3%. Yet at the point 8 years after entry, the prestige scores of whites are only a little more predictable than those of blacks (47.8% versus 43.9%), and black wage values proved to be *more* predictable (31.6% versus 37.4%). So, blacks are less able to convert the characteristics of their families and additional education into better first jobs. But by the point 2 years after entry much of the difference in the predictability of white and black occupational levels has disappeared. Thus, it is not sufficient to describe racial differences simply in terms of the mean levels of jobs held—the amount of uncertainty in the process is also an important factor. The result of the lower education and first job variances is to handicap the black individual from a more middle-class background or with more schooling; he cannot be as certain to obtain good jobs as his white counterpart—and of course this uncertainty is coupled with lower average outcomes.

Do the large number of racial differences observed constitute grounds for arguing that blacks are not merely disadvantaged when compared to whites, but that the stratification *process*—as evidenced by the relationships among its component variables—differs fundamentally for the two races? It is difficult to give an unequivocal answer, but our inclination is to answer in the negative, to conclude that the most important factors separating blacks and whites are levels of family background and education. Yet at each point of the analysis, what happens to whites and blacks is not quite the same, and in each transition in the chain of events—from family background to education, from education to the first job, from the first job to the one held 2 years after entry and then to the job held 8 years after entry—the deficit increases. Blacks do not get as much out of their education or their first jobs as whites. We are never quite successful in attributing all of the racial differences at any one point to prior deficits. But there is an overall similarity, the relative contributions of the separate components of the stratification process do not markedly differ. Indeed, the relatively large differences in these relationships, found in the analysis of the first job after entry, are substantially reduced in the next 8 years. Our conclusion is that the careers of blacks and whites operate within a common stratification system, but that its parameters are somewhat different for the two races, and these differences within the overall process account for the continual worsening of the relative positions of blacks.

THE ROLE OF FAMILY BACKGROUND

The only part of the stratification process in which family background has been shown to play a *direct* role is in determining the amount of education with which men enter the labor force. Its influence on all the later steps in the process is mostly channeled through education, though a number of small direct effects do appear. Family background explains about 10% of the variation in the prestige scores and wages of jobs held after entry (at the zero-order level), through the variance explained varies according to the measure used, race, and the time of the job. If we are prepared to see family background as a prior cause and to attribute all of its indirect effects back to this group of four variables, then family background explains between one-quarter and one-third of the variation in job outcomes; in most cases this turns out to be about one-half as great as the impact of education (if it too is inserted in the regression in temporal order). Family background is usually the second most important determinant of the prestige and wage variables examined here. It has a stronger effect on education than on prestige scores, and a stronger effect on prestige scores than on wages.

EDUCATION, OCCUPATIONAL PRESTIGE, AND WAGES

Much of this study has dealt with the relationships among educational attainment, occupational prestige scores, and wages. Table 6.2 contains differences between the mean prestige scores and wage values of high school graduates and men with no high school, and also between college and high school graduates; for the first job and for the points 1, 2, and 8 years after entry. Again the differences are measured in units of standard deviations of the variables. There is considerable fluctuation in the prestige differences, but, except for the gap between black college and high school graduates, the differences between men of different educational levels increase between the first job and the point 8 years after entry. The opposite is true of wages. After 8 years of work, the differences in wages between high school graduates and men with no high school, and between college and high school graduates, are smaller than they are for the first job.

It is also apparent that educational attainment serves to create greater gaps in prestige scores than it does in wages. Taking the values for whites and using the job 8 years after entry, the difference in the average

TABLE 6.2 MEAN DIFFERENCE BETWEEN HIGH SCHOOL GRADUATES AND MEN WITH NO HIGH SCHOOL AND BETWEEN COLLEGE AND HIGH SCHOOL GRADUATES, FOR IMPORTANT STRATIFICATION VARIABLES BY RACE, ALL MEASURED IN UNITS OF STANDARD DEVIATIONS OF THE VARIABLE

Variable	Difference between the Mean Values of High School Graduates and Men with No High School		Difference between the Mean Values of College and High School Graduates	
	White	Black	White	Black
Occupational Prestige				
First job after entry	.47	.52	1.48	1.40
One year after entry	.61	.73	1.59	1.32
Two years after entry	.69	.79	1.54	1.57
Eight years after entry	.64	.67	1.37	1.74
Wages				
First job after entry	.74	.66	.77	.60
One year after entry	.77	.74	.81	.60
Two years after entry	.56	.77	.71	.73
Eight years after entry	.51	.50	.71	.54

prestige scores of high school graduates amounts to .64 standard deviations of prestige, while the corresponding difference for wages is .51. The contrast between prestige and wages is more marked when we consider the gap between college and high school graduates, which amounts to 1.37 standard deviations for prestige, .71 for wages. This is a very considerable difference; it means that while there is little overlap in the prestige distributions of high school and college graduates, considerable numbers of high school graduates make as much money as some of the college graduates. So, one reason why blacks are in a relatively worse position in terms of prestige than they are in wages is because their lower levels of education have less impact on wages. The path diagrams clearly show how educational attainment has a stronger effect on prestige. After 8 years in the labor force, the direct effect of education on wages is close to zero—its impact flowing entirely through the wage of the first job (which *was* directly affected by education). Education directly affects the occupational prestige score throughout the period studied.

The magnitude of the relationships among these three variables has strong implications for the nature of mobility after entry. Wage values are strongly tied to earlier wages, but their direct connection to educational attainment is weak; the best predictor of occupational prestige is education, and the prestige scores of earlier jobs are not so important. The result is that individuals with higher levels of education can expect to experience greater prestige mobility, but there is no such single important predictor of wage mobility (at least none that was included among our variables)—and later wages are limited by the wage of the first job after entry. Of course, while these patterns hold for an 8-year period after entry, they may change later in men's careers. Once a man has entered the labor force, his education at entry explains about 80% of the variation in education 8 years later for whites, and 90% of it for blacks. The educational mobility that does take place cannot be properly predicted by any of the variables we have used to describe the stratification process.

MODELS OF THE STRATIFICATION PROCESS, AND THE ROLE OF OTHER VARIABLES

Researchers whose primary interest is in the labor force have concentrated their attention on quite different aspects of entry into the labor force than have sociologists working on models of the stratification system as a whole. While the former have examined the industries of jobs and how they are located, unemployment and labor force participation, sociologists have usually been content to take a single first job and measure it with a socioeconomic score. These concerns reflect the different interests and intellectual priorities of labor economists and sociologists. In this study we have taken some of the variables used in labor force studies and assessed their impact on the levels of jobs obtained. For example, instead of the usual concern with the effectiveness of various methods of finding jobs as measured by whether or not an individual succeeds in *finding* a job, we have used regression analysis to discover whether the method used to find a job has any impact on the *level* of the job that is found. We have taken a number of variables that are usually dealt with in a very descriptive fashion and integrated them into a framework of research in social stratification that deals conventionally with measures of educational attainment, father's education and occupation, and so on.

What are the implications of our findings for the success of the relatively simplified models sociologists now construct? The new variables we have included, such as pre-entry job experiences, moves, and marital status, do *not* fundamentally alter the relationships among family background, educational attainment, and job prestige. The two modifications to these models that are suggested by this research do not involve the addition of such variables as industry. We suggest that wages, measured at entry as well as later in the career, be included, and that educational attainment be allowed to change after entry. The dynamics of wage mobility are quite different from those of prestige (and thus of socioeconomic rankings, which behave in a similar fashion). If the entry process is to be properly represented in stratification models, the substantial educational changes after entry must be included; or, alternatively, a definition of entry should be established which ensures that very little educational change can take place after the first job.

We have examined both the numbers and the levels of jobs held before entry. Whites hold many more such jobs, both full-time and part-time, even when educational attainment and age at entry are held constant. The jobs held by whites have higher prestige scores and slightly higher wages than those of blacks, though the range of both these variables is very limited. Whatever these patterns, the analysis of jobs held after entry shows that these pre-entry work experiences have little long-term impact. The one consistent finding is that whites with one or more jobs before entering the labor force have slightly higher wages, both in the first job and in the job held 8 years after entry. Not only do fewer blacks hold such jobs but the ones who do receive little long-term benefit from them. There is no consistent relationship between pre-entry work experience and later prestige scores, and it is possible that the net impact of pre-entry experience on later occupational achievement is negative. In any event, the impact cannot be large. It is likely that many of the jobs held before entry are taken because of economic need, and they cannot generally be taken as indicators of ambition and confidence in the young worker. They do however appear to give him a claim to slightly higher wages, or perhaps they make him more concerned with getting more pay.

The industry of a job, measured in six crude categories, does have a measurable effect on both prestige scores and wages. The five dummy variables uniquely explain as much as 7% or 8% of the variance in prestige scores, but considerably less for wages. This is not surprising, since the occupational composition of the six industrial categories varies considerably. The two interesting findings are that the industrial differences remain quite large even when the respondent's educational attainment, family background, and a number of other variables are held constant; and second, that the ordering of the industries varies markedly according to the object of prediction is prestige or wages. This fact makes it difficult for the job-seeker, when choosing an industry in which to look for a job or exploring the industries in which openings exist, to simultaneously maximize these two measures of job quality. We find that the category of industry does much more to determine the kind of work a person does, at least insofar as this is measured by the prestige score, than what a man gets paid for that work. And we find that the industry of a job has little impact beyond the duration of that job.

Moves made between entry into the labor force and the start of the first job, the respondent's marital status, and the method used to locate a given job all have small effects on the prestige scores and wages of jobs. Their size varies according to which of the two measures of job quality is used, and the point that has been reached in the individual's career. Generally, moves increase wages but have little effect on prestige scores; married men have higher wages; and jobs into which a man is promoted or which he finds for himself (rather than with the help of his family or friends) have both higher prestige scores and wages. None of these variables has much of an overall effect on the level of jobs held, and our estimates are subject to considerable random fluctuation because of the small numbers of cases in the sample. It is sometimes difficult to predict or to interpret the results that are obtained. For example, it makes sense that whites who locate the jobs they hold 8 years after entry by "direct" methods should have better jobs, since presumably these individuals have a wider range of choice than those who relied on personal friends and relatives. But why should there be no such difference for blacks—since one can only assume that relying on personal contacts would do even more in their case to restrict the choice of jobs? Perhaps job discrimination is the cause.

A sample such as the one used here is certainly large enough to yield rough estimates of the impact of such variables as these and to bring out any large effects. However, it is not large enough to produce very accurate estimates, or even to determine the approximate size, of the differences produced by variables with very weak effects. To take one example, only about 80 whites and 80 blacks moved between entry and the start of their first job. We have succeeded in showing that the impact of moving is not very large, but perhaps the direction of the move is critical—moves into certain cities or between particular regions might yield very large payoffs. A larger sample would be required to deal effectively with these questions.

About one-half of all respondents served in the armed forces at some time in the 8 years after they entered the labor force. The *net* effect of military service on an individual's subsequent jobs is very small, though for particular groups it may have moderate effects. College graduates who serve in the armed forces suffer a prestige loss of about 7 points. We can summarize by saying that veterans with little education gain small amounts of prestige; that black veterans have higher wages and white veterans lower wages than nonveterans of the same race with equal education and that magnitude of these differences increases with education; that veterans are slightly more likely than nonveterans to increase their education after entry. The only important net result of these effects is that white veterans suffer a small loss of wages. There are no important prestige differences. Of course, these results apply only when education, family background, first job, pre-entry job experiences, and the nature of the job held 8 years after entry are all held constant. The untangling of these effects is a small analytic puzzle, since the effect of military service interacts with both race and education and is different for the prestige and wage variables!

FURTHER RESEARCH

The most obvious ways in which to build on the results that have been presented here are to expand the analysis of entry into the labor force to include women and to add measures of the entrants' perceptions of themselves. The case for including women needs no elaboration. Sewell and others have shown that the level of an individual's aspirations plays an important intervening role within the stratification process. The addition of some measures of intelligence, or perhaps of early school grades, would also be important.

Many of the issues could be treated in much greater detail, and in some cases these data could be used to do this. For example, a more precise analysis of migration is possible—since the location of the respondent is recorded at each point in time, it is possible to compare movement from the countryside to the nearest city with moves across regions, and so on. But certain analyses are impossible because the sample used here is too small. Nor is there any way to obtain precise results from the mere 25 black entrants with college degrees. Ideally, one could imagine a very large sample with approximately equal numbers of male and female and white and black respondents at each of five or six levels of education. Then it would be possible to examine each separate group in the way in which whites and blacks were treated here, and the subsamples could be combined, using the appropriate weights, whenever that was desired. There is no doubt that the collection of such a large body of data would be very costly.

Finally, there is one intellectual imperative which we touched on in the review of the literature in the first chapter. The challenge that must eventually be faced is to combine the analysis of individual careers—the mode of this study—with data on the labor market as a whole. As we have pointed out, the 60% of the variation in careers that cannot be explained using individual characteristics is by no means inexplicable. When a person enters the labor market, he or she has only a certain range of alternatives; an individual can only choose among the job openings that do exist, at the rates of pay offered by the employers with jobs. As has recently become apparent, a massive increase in the number of individuals with college degrees is more likely to result in their being forced to take jobs formerly held by people with much less education than in some magical transformation of the occupational structure so as to accommodate what might have been the reasonable expectations of college graduates 10 years ago. These are not immeasurables, labor economists have traditionally been concerned with variations in the wage rates of geographic areas and among firms, and the structure of the labor force is very well known. By bringing them together it should be possible to account for all of the variation in careers, and to allocate it to individual and institutional factors.

Appendix A

Survey 4068
January, 1969

NATIONAL OPINION RESEARCH CENTER
University of Chicago

LIFE CIRCUMSTANCES STUDY

TIME BEGAN: 7:00 ~~AM~~ PM

Segment Number: 654-321

DULS Line Number: 12

Street Address: 123 Vickers Road

City and State: Hampstead, Long Island, N.Y.

INTRODUCTION

This is a study to find out how early events in life may affect later events.

I am going to ask you when certain things occurred in your life, beginning when you were fourteen years old. As we talk, you will probably think of other things which have happened to you. Even some which you might think are not important, we would like to know about.

I have a year-by-year calendar on which to record when these events took place. Sometimes when you are not able to remember the exact year, you may be able to tell me how old you were at the time, or what else happened to you at the same time.

Information of this kind will help us obtain the correct dates and a complete picture of your life.

First, how old were you on your birthday in 1968, and when was your birthday?

39   January 6, 1929
(Age)   (Birth date)

TEAR AGE STRIP SO THAT AGE IN 1968 IS AT THE BOTTOM OF STRIP. AFFIX AGE STRIP TO PAGE 2 SO THAT AGE IN 1968 APPEARS NEXT TO "1968."

INTERVIEWER: ALWAYS INDICATE STOPPING POINT BY END OF ARROW.

		\[1. FULL-TIME EDUCATION\]			\[2. FULL-TIME EMPLOYMENT OR UNEMPLOYMENT (Ask 11-a "Support," for unempl.)\]		
		(a)	(b)	(c) Degree/ highest	(a)	(b)	(c)
Year	Age	Month	Name and/or type of school	gr.comp.	Month	Occupation	Industry
1943	14		Barker Elem.				
1944	15	June Sept	Barker Cons. HS	8 9			
1945	16	June Sept	St. Louis Public HS #5	10			
1946	17	Sept	↓ Oct	10	Nov Dec	Unemployed (see note p. 3) Attendant	Gas Station ↓
1947	18				Apr-July	Stock Clerk	Dept. Store
1948	19					Army (see 5.)	
1949	20						
1950	21						
1951	22				Feb	Driver	City Bus Co.
1952	23					↓	
1953	24	Sept	City College of New York		Aug	↓	↓
1954	25						
1955	26	June	↓	BA (business)	June	Salesman	Levin Bros. Soap Mfg.
1956	27						
1957	28					↓	↓
1958	29				Aug	Area Supervisor	O. Sedar Brush Co.
1959	30						
1960	31						
1961	32						
1962	33						
1963	34						
1964	35				Feb	↓	
1965	36				March	Office Manager	
1966	37						
1967	38						
1968	39					↓	↓
Current						Office Manager	O. Sedar Brush

Wages (d) In $ Beg. Amt.	End'g Amt.	(e) In kind F=food H=hous'g	(f) Hrs/wk	(g) Left Job: O=own decision N=not own decision	(h) At termination: H=had new job K=knew of job N=neither	(i) Got Job thru: Fr=Friends Fa=Family Pu=Pub.ag. Pr=Priv.ag. A=Ads O=Other	(j) On-the-Job Training (incl. apprentice trng.) How long? Never? [ ]
.75 hr			40			A	
	.75hr			N	N		
.80 hr	.80		40	N	N	Pu	
1.10 hr			40			A	Driver Training 3 weeks
	1.30 hr		40	O	N (see note)		
$6,000 yr			42			O	Management Training Program - 6 weeks
	$7,500 yr		40	O	H		
$8,250 yr			40-45			O	
	$11,000 yr		40-45	N	N		
			leave of absence for illness				
$12,000 yr			45-50			back to same job	
Co. $13,000 yr			45-50				

USE THIS PAGE FOR EXTRA NOTATIONS BUT ALWAYS INDICATE YEAR AND COLUMN TO WHICH NOTE APPLIES.

Year	
1943	Col. 12 - R not sure if actual rent was paid or part of sharecropper arrangement
1944	
1945	
1946	
1947	
1948	
1949	
1950	
1951	Col. 4 - R was half-time student for a few years, worked toward B.A.
1952	
1953	
1954	
1955	
1956	
1957	
1958	
1959	
1960	
1961	
1962	
1963	
1964	
1965	
1966	
1967	
1968	
Current	

190

INTERVIEWER: ALWAYS INDICATE STOPPING POINT BY END OF ARROW.

USE 2-A ONLY IF R HAD MORE THAN TWO JOBS IN GIVEN YEAR & ALWAYS GO BACK TO P.2 FOR NEXT YEAR.

2-A
FULL TIME EMPLOYMENT OR UNEMPLOYMENT:
(Ask 11-a "Support," for unempl.)

(k) Name of Union — Never? [X]

(a) Month	(b) Occupation	(c) Industry	(d) Wages In $ Beg. Amt.	(d) Wages In $ End'g Amt.	(e) In kind P=food H=hous'g	(f) hrs/ wk	(g) Left Job: O=own decision N=not own decision	(h) At termination: H=had new job K=knew of job N=neither	(i) Got Job thru: Fr=Friends Fa=Family Pu=Pub.ag. Pr=Priv.ag. A=Ads O=Other	(j) On-the-Job Training (incl. apprentice trng.) How long? Never? [ ]	(k) Name of Union Never? [ ]	Year
Jul-Sept	Ice Cream Seller (walking cart)	Dairy-Ice Co.	$50 wk	$60 wk (got commission)		50	est O	K	Fr			1947
Sept-Dec	Laborer	Hiway Const. Co.	$1 hr	$1 hr		40	N	N	Pu			1947

NOTES

Nov. 1946   R looked for work without success after quitting school. He dropped out after repeating 10th grade for a month.

Aug. 1953   R stopped working full-time for Bus Co. in order to give full time to his studies, but cont'd to drive bus on a part-time basis.

INTERVIEWER: ALWAYS INDICATE STOPPING POINT BY END OF ARROW.

					PART-TIME EDUCATION:	
	3. PART-TIME EMPLOYMENT: Never? ☐				Never? ☐	
(a)	(b)	(c)	(d)	(e)	(a) Name and/or	(b)
Month	Occupation	Industry	Wages	Hrs/wk	type of school	Month
					City College of New York	Sept.
Sept.	Bus Driver	City Bus Co.	$1.30 hr	30		Aug.
Feb.			$1.40 hr	20		
Feb.–May	Library Asst.	Univ. Library	$1.25 hr	25		

4. (c) Degree/ Diploma/ Certificate or Course	(d) Tuition R=Self E=Empl. O=Other	5. MILITARY SERVICE: (a) Draf./Enl. Long. Stay Pl. of Dis.	(b) Beginning & ending rank	Never? ☐ (c) Education Never? ☐	6. OTHER FULL-TIME ACTIVITIES: Major illnesses? Travel? Etc.?	Year
						1943
						1944
						1945
						1946
		Dec.-	Priv.			1947
		drafted		G.E.D. H.S.diploma		1948
		Georgia				1949
		Dec.-Mo.	Corporal			1950
Business Major	0	Ft. Leonard Wood				1951
	0					1952
	0					1953
						1954
						1955
						1956
						1957
						1958
						1959
						1960
						1961
						1962
						1963
					Feb.-Tuberculosis	1964
					↓ March	1965
						1966
						1967
						1968
						Current

INTERVIEWER: ALWAYS INDICATE STOPPING POINT BY END OF ARROW.

Year	7. FAMILY HISTORY (a) Month & Marital Status	(b) Wife's age at marriage	(c) Children M=male F=female Mo.of birth	(d) Birth control dur.mar. Never?	8. WIFE'S EDUCATION Degree or highest gr.comp. at mar.&since	9. WIFE'S EMPLOYMENT (during marriage to R.): Never? (a) Month	(b) Occupation	(c) Industry	(d) Wages	(e) Hrs/wk
1943										
1944										
1945										
1946	Nov married	16		no	10th gr					
1947			M-July							
1948						Jan	Cleaning Lady	Gov't Hosp.	.65 hr .80 hr	40
1949						Dec	Sales Clerk	10¢ Store	.95 hr	40
1950	↓									
1951	June divorce			↓		June	↓	↓	↓	↓
1952										
1953										
1954										
1955	↓									
1956	July married	23		yes	A.B.	July	Journalist	Daily News Paper	$5,000 yr	40
1957				no						
1958			F-May	-		Feb	↓	↓	$5,250 yr	40
1959			F-Sept	-						
1960				yes						
1961										
1962										
1963										
1964						Sept	Journalist	Daily News Paper	$7,500 yr	35
1965										
1966										
1967										
1968	↓									
Current	married			↓			↓	↓	$9,500	↓

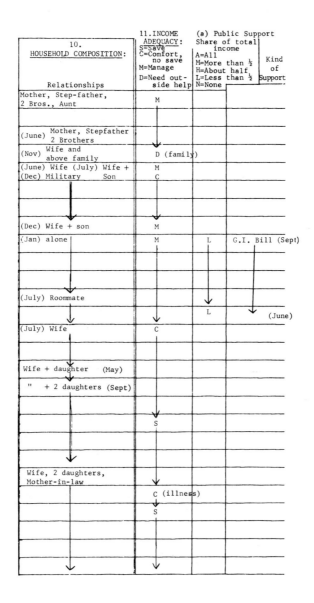

10. HOUSEHOLD COMPOSITION: Relationships	11. INCOME ADEQUACY: S=Save C=Comfort, no save M=Manage D=Need outside help	(a) Public Support Share of total income A=All M=More than ½ H=About half L=Less than ½ N=None	Kind of Support
Mother, Step-father, 2 Bros., Aunt	M		
(June) Mother, Stepfather 2 Brothers			
(Nov) Wife and above family	D (family)		
(June) Wife (July) Wife + (Dec) Military Son	M C		
(Dec) Wife + son	M		
(Jan) alone	M	L	G.I. Bill (Sept)
(July) Roommate		L	
			(June)
(July) Wife	C		
Wife + daughter (May)			
" + 2 daughters (Sept)			
	S		
Wife, 2 daughters, Mother-in-law			
	C (illness)		
	S		

<u>INTERVIEWER</u>: ALWAYS INDICATE STOPPING POINT BY END OF ARROW.

12. HOME DETAILS				(e) Neighborhood	13.	
(a)	(b)	(c)	(d)	AW=all white	WHERE LIVING	
			Own/Rent/	MW=mostly white HH=about ½ & ½	(a)	(b)
		#	Share-no	MNW=mostly non-wh.		
Month	Type	Rooms	rent	ANW=all non-white	City/Town	County
	House	3	R *see p.4	Rural - no neighborhood	---	Barker
June	Apt.	4	R	ANW	St. Louis	
June Dec.	Apt. Barracks	2 -	R -	ANW -	Army	
Dec.	Apt.	3	R	ANW	St. Louis	Barker
Jan.	Apt.	1	R	ANW	Newark	-
June	Apt.	1	R	HH	New York	
July	Apt.	2	R	HH		
May	Apt.	4	R	MW		
Oct.	House	7	O	MW	Hampstead	Long Island Nassau
				HH		

(c) State	(d) RF RNF	(e) Month	Year
Miss.	RF		1943
			1944
Mo.		June	1945
			1946
		Dec.	1947
			1948
			1949
Mo.		Dec.	1950
NJ NY		Jan. June	1951
			1952
			1953
			1954
			1955
			1956
			1957
			1958
			1959
NY		Oct.	1960
			1961
			1962
			1963
			1964
			1965
			1966
			1967
			1968
			Current

We've asked you about your life history in the preceding questions. Now we have some general questions about your background.

14. Where were you born?

    Milk Junction   Barker   Mississippi
    (City/Town)   (County)   (State)

    IF FOREIGN BORN: In what year did you come to this country?
                                    19 --

15. How many brothers and sisters did you or do you have, all told?

    __2__ Brothers   __0__ Sisters

16. A. What was the last year of schooling that your father completed?

    3rd Grade

    (If Education is for father substitute, check [X] and specify relationship:

    Step-father   )

    B. What was the last year of schooling that your mother completed?

    6th Grade

17. A. When you were 14, what kind of work did your father do?

    OCCUPATION: Sharecropper (laborer)

    INDUSTRY: Agriculture - cotton

    (If occupation is for father substitute, check [X] and specify relationship:

    Step-father   )

    IF NO FATHER & NO SUB. AT R'S AGE 14, CHECK BOX [ ]

    B. What kind of work did your mother do, when you were 14?

    OCCUPATION: Domestic

    INDUSTRY: Private homes

18. Around the time you were 14, would you say your family was:

    Very happy   [ ]
    Somewhat happy   [ ]
    Somewhat unhappy   [X]
    Very unhappy   [ ]

19. ASK FOR WHITES ONLY:

A. What is the main nationality in your mother's background?

Baptist

B. What is the main nationality in your father's background?

_____

20. A. In what religion were you brought up?

Baptist

B. Is (religion in A) your religion now, or do you have a different religion now?

Same ☐   Different ☒

IF DIFFERENT NOW:

C. What is your religion now? _Episcopalian_

D. When did you change? 19 _56_

21. Did you vote in the **last Presidential** election?   Yes ☒   No ☐

IF YES:
A. For whom did you vote?

Humphrey

22. What was the year of the _first election_ in which you voted?   19 _52_

(Check box ☐ if never voted.)

23. A. In thinking back about your life, what are the major things, good or bad, that have happened in your life which changed it in a way you did not expect? What other major things changed your life in a way you didn't expect? (PROBE: How did that change your life?

B. INTERVIEWER: AFTER RECORDING R'S RESPONSES IN A, CROSS THRU IN BOX EACH OF THE "LIFE AREAS" HE MENTIONED; THEN ASK Q. 23 SPECIFICALLY FOR EACH "LIFE AREA" NOT YET MENTIONED.

Life Areas to be covered:
Family life
Job/career
Education
Military (unless had none)
Major moves

The Army X I began to see a lot of different places and

different kinds of people X I learned the importance of being

educated and finished H.S., then I went to college on the G.I.

Bill.

My second marriage X She had always had advantages X She

helped me to live with other people X Well, not being so mad

about my own lousy childhood X and she's great to live with

X The crucial point was when the man from O. Sedar offered me a

job. He knew I wasn't moving up fast enough at Levier Bros. X The best

thing about moving was getting out of Mississippi X that's all.

24. We would like to know something about how people go about guessing words that they do not know. HAND RESPONDENT CARD. On this card are listed some words--you may know some of them and you may not know quite a few of them.

On each line there is a word in capital letters--like BEAST. Then there are five other words. Tell me the number of the word that comes closest to the meaning of the word in capital letters. If the word in capital letters is BEAST, you would say "4" since "animal" comes closer to "beast" than any of the other words. If you wish, I will read the words to you. These words are difficult for almost everyone--give me your best guess if you're not sure of the answer. CIRCLE THE ANSWER GIVEN BELOW.

SPACE	1 school	2 noon	3 captain	④ room	5 board	9 NA
BROADEN	1 efface	2 make level	3 elapse	4 embroider	⑤ widen	9 NA
CAPRICE	1 value	2 a star	3 grimace	② whim	5 inducement	9 NA
EDIBLE	1 auspicious	2 eligible	③ fit to eat	4 sagacious	5 able to speak	9 NA
ANIMOSITY	① hatred	2 animation	3 disobedience	4 diversity	5 friendship	9 NA
PACT	1 puissance	2 remonstrance	③ agreement	4 skillet	5 pressure	9 NA
CLOISTERED	1 miniature	② bunched	3 arched	4 malady	5 secluded	9 NA
EMANATE	① rival	2 come	3 prominent	4 free	5 populate	9 NA
ACCUSTOM	1 disappoint	2 customary	3 encounter	④ get used to	5 business	9 NA
ALLUSION	1 reference	2 dream	3 eulogy	④ illusion	5 aria	9 NA

INTERVIEWER: CHECK ONE BOX BELOW:

R read words in Q. 24 himself [X]

You read words in Q. 24 to him [ ]

25. Social Security Number:

636-84-4026

199

That's the end of the interview. Thank you very much. You have been most helpful. I'd like to record your full name, address, and telephone number in case my office wants to verify this interview.

Harold Faulkner
(Name)

123 Vickers Road
(Street)

Hampstead   N.Y.
(City)   (State)

212 123-4567
(Telephone No., include area code)

S. S. Permission   Yes [X]
                     No [ ]

Time Ended: 8:10   xAMxx
                         PM

Total length of interview: 70   minutes

IMPORTANT - FILL IN THE ITEMS BELOW IMMEDIATELY AFTER LEAVING RESPONDENT

A. On the basis of your observation, rate the respondent and his home using the 4-point scale.

RESPONDENT IN INTERVIEW SITUATION:

Friendly	1	(2)	3	4 Hostile
Specific	(1)	2	3	4 Vague
Relaxed	1	(2)	3	4 Tense
Cooperative	(1)	2	3	4 Uncooperative
Interested	1	(2)	3	4 Not interested

FURNISHINGS IN RESPONDENT'S HOME:

Excellent quality	1	(2)	3	4 Poor quality
Excellent condition	I	(2)	3	4 Poor condition

B. Neighborhood description. CHECK ONE OF THE FOLLOWING:

[ ] A wealthy, or "society"-type neighborhood; top business executives, prominent lawyers and doctors, and people with inherited incomes live here.

[ ] A very well-to-do white-collar neighborhood--doctors, highly paid managers; strictly a professional and executive neighborhood.

[X] A good white-collar neighborhood--not many executives or doctors live here, but there are probably no blue-collar people, either.

[ ] Predominantly white-collar neighborhood, though a lot of fairly well-paid blue-collar families live here also.

[ ] Predominantly a blue-collar neighborhood--though some office workers might live here also.

[ ] Strictly a working-class neighborhood; probably no white-collar workers live here.

[ ] A neighborhood of laborers and unemployed.

[ ] Rural farming area--houses are far apart; farmers appear to be prosperous.

[ ] Rural farming area--houses are far apart; farmers appear to be having hard time making ends meet.

C. Respondent's race:

White	1
Black	(2)
Other (SPECIFY) . . .	3

D. CHECK BOX FOR ONE SENTENCE BELOW.

[X] Respondent's wife was present but did not participate in interview.

[ ] Respondent's wife participated but only with information about herself.

[ ] Respondent's wife participated with information about herself and also helped R to remember information about himself.

[ ] Respondent's wife was not present.

[ ] Respondent is not married.

[ ] Other person(s) present (SPECIFY)

INTERVIEWER'S SIGNATURE: Dolly Clipboard

DATE OF INTERVIEW: 12-28-68

Appendix B

*From James Murray, "Continuous National Survey," NORC Report No.125, July 1974
(National Opinion Research Center, University of Chicago).

```
                INSURANCE AND REAL ESTATE                             53.2
                AUTOMOBILE REPAIR SERVICES AND GARAGES                39.2
                MISCELLANEOUS REPAIR SERVICES                         29.0
                BUSINESS AND PERSONAL SERVICES                        52.6
                ALL OTHER INDUSTRIES (INCLUDING NOT REPORTED)         50.3
        CLERICAL AND KINDRED WORKERS                                  39.4
                AGENTS NEC                                            42.5
                ATTENDANTS AND ASSISTANTS, LIBRARY                    41.3
                ATTENDANTS, PHYSICIAN'S AND DENTIST'S OFFICE          47.8
                BAGGAGEMEN, TRANSPORTATION                            23.2
                BANK TELLERS                                          49.5
                BOOKKEEPERS                                           47.6
                CASHIERS                                              30.9
                COLLECTORS, BILL AND ACCOUNT                          25.9
                DISPATCHERS AND STARTERS, VEHICLE                     33.5
                EXPRESS MESSENGERS AND RAILWAY MAIL CLERKS            37.6
                FILE CLERKS                                           30.3
                INSURANCE ADJUSTERS, EXAMINERS, AND INVESTIGATORS     47.7
                MAIL CARRIERS                                         42.3
                MESSENGERS AND OFFICE BOYS                            19.1
                OFFICE MACHINE OPERATORS                              44.9
                PAYROLL AND TIMEKEEPING CLERKS                        41.3
                POSTAL CLERKS                                         43.0
                RECEPTIONISTS                                         39.4
                SECRETARIES                                           45.8
                SHIPPING AND RECEIVING CLERKS                         29.2
                STENOGRAPHERS                                         43.3
                STOCK CLERKS AND STOREKEEPERS                         23.4
                TELEGRAPH MESSENGERS                                  29.8
                TELEGRAPH OPERATORS                                   43.5
                TELEPHONE OPERATORS                                   40.4
                TICKET, STATION, AND EXPRESS AGENTS                   35.4
                TYPISTS                                               41.3
                CLERICAL AND KINDRED WORKERS, NEC                     36.2
        SALES WORKERS                                                 33.6
                ADVERTISING AGENTS AND SALESMEN                       42.2
                AUCTIONEERS                                           31.9
                DEMONSTRATORS                                         28.3
                HUCKSTERS AND PEDDLERS                                18.3
                INSURANCE AGENTS, BROKERS, AND UNDERWRITERS           46.8
                NEWSBOYS                                              15.4
                REAL ESTATE AGENTS AND BROKERS                        44.0
                STOCK, BOND SALESMEN                                  50.6
                SALESMEN AND SALES CLERKS, NEC                        32.8
                 MANUFACTURING                                        49.1
                 WHOLESALE TRADE                                      39.9
                 RETAIL TRADE                                         28.6
                 OTHER INDUSTRIES (INCLUDING NOT REPORTED)            33.8
        CRAFTSMEN, FOREMEN, AND KINDRED WORKERS                       38.8
                BAKERS                                                34.2
                BLACKSMITHS                                           35.5
                BOILERMAKERS                                          30.7
                BOOKBINDERS                                           31.3
                BRICK MASONS, STONE MASONS, AND TILE SETTERS          35.7
                CABINETMAKERS                                         38.6
                CARPENTERS                                            39.9
                CEMENT AND CONCRETE FINISHERS                         31.6
                COMPOSITORS AND TYPESETTERS                           38.0
                CRANEMEN, DERRICKMEN, AND HOISTMEN                    38.8
                DECORATORS AND WINDOW DRESSERS                        37.4
                ELECTRICIANS                                          49.2
                ELECTROTYPERS AND STEREOTYPERS                        38.0
                ENGRAVERS, EXCEPT PHOTOENGRAVERS                      41.2
                EXCAVATING, GRADING, AND ROAD MACHINERY OPERATORS     32.6
                FOREMEN, NEC                                          45.3
                 CONSTRUCTION                                         46.1
                 MANUFACTURING                                        45.1
                 ALL OTHER INDUSTRIES                                 45.6
                FORGEMEN AND HAMMERMEN                                35.5
```

```
MEAT CUTTERS, EXCEPT SLAUGHTER AND PACKING HOUSE              32.1
MILLINERS                                                    33.4
MINE OPERATIVES AND LABORERS                                 26.3
 COAL MINING                                                 25.2
 CRUDE PETROLEUM AND NATURAL GAS EXTRACTION                  28.4
 MINING AND QUARRYING, EXCEPT FUEL                           25.8
MOTORMEN, MINE, FACTORY, LOGGING CAMP, ETC                   27.2
MOTORMEN, STREET, SUBWAY, AND ELEVATED RAILWAY               28.0
OILERS AND GREASERS, EXCEPT AUTO                             24.2
PACKERS AND WRAPPERS, NEC                                    19.4
PAINTERS, EXCEPT CONSTRUCTION AND MAINTENANCE                29.0
PHOTOGRAPHIC PROCESS WORKERS                                 35.9
POWER STATION OPERATORS                                      38.8
SAILORS AND DECK HANDS                                       33.7
SAWYERS                                                      27.7
SEWERS AND STITCHERS, MANUFACTURING                          24.9
SPINNERS, TEXTILE                                            24.9
STATIONARY FIREMAN                                           32.5
SWITCHMEN, RAILROAD                                          32.8
TAXICAB DRIVERS AND CHAUFFEURS                               21.5
TRUCK AND TRACTOR DRIVERS                                    32.1
WEAVERS, TEXTILE                                             24.9
WELDERS AND FLAME-CUTTERS                                    40.1
OPERATIVES AND KINDRED WORKERS, NEC                          29.0
 MANUFACTURING                                               29.0
  DURABLE GOODS                                              30.7
  SAWMILLS, PLANING MILLS, AND MISCELLANEOUS WOOD
   PRODUCTS                                                  23.6
  FURNITURE AND FIXTURES                                     27.6
  STONE, CLAY, AND GLASS PRODUCTS                            23.1
  METAL INDUSTRIES                                           29.5
   PRIMARY METAL INDUSTRIES                                  34.7
   FABRICATED METAL INDUSTRIES, INCLUDING
    NOT SPECIFIED METAL
                                                             25.0
  MACHINERY, EXCEPT ELECTRICAL                               30.4
  ELECTRICAL MACHINERY, EQUIPMENT AND SUPPLIES               38.6
  TRANSPORTATION EQUIPMENT                                   33.4
   MOTOR VEHICLES AND MOTOR VEHICLE EQUIPMENT                30.8
   AIRCRAFT AND PARTS                                        41.9
   SHIP AND BOAT BUILDING AND REPAIRING                      30.8
   RAILROAD AND MISCELLANEOUS TRANSPORTATION EQUIPMENT       24.9
  PROFESSIONAL AND PHOTOGRAPHIC EQUIPMENT AND WATCHES        30.3
  MISCELLANEOUS MANUFACTURING INDUSTRIES                     31.6
 NONDURABLE GOODS                                            27.5
  FOOD AND KINDRED PRODUCTS                                  23.0
  TOBACCO MANUFACTURERS                                      24.8
  TEXTILE MILL PRODUCTS                                      28.8
  APPAREL AND OTHER FABRICATED TEXTILE PRODUCTS              25.8
  PAPER AND ALLIED PRODUCTS                                  24.8
  PRINTING, PUBLISHING AND ALLIED INDUSTRIES                 33.1
  CHEMICALS AND ALLIED PRODUCTS                              31.9
  PETROLEUM AND COAL PRODUCTS                                30.6
  RUBBER AND MISCELLANEOUS PLASTIC PRODUCTS                  29.8
  LEATHER AND LEATHER PRODUCTS                               31.6
 NOT SPECIFIED MANUFACTURING INDUSTRIES                      31.6
 NON-MANUFACTURING INDUSTRIES (INCLUDING NOT REPORTED)       28.9
 SALES                                                       50.6
 CONSTRUCTION                                                27.4
 TRANSPORTATION, COMMUNICATIONS, AND UTILITIES AND
  SANITARY SERVICES (INCLUDING RAILROADS)                    33.1
 WHOLESALE AND RETAIL TRADE, AND BUSINESS, REPAIR, AND
  PERSONAL SERVICES                                          25.9
 PUBLIC ADMINISTRATION                                       33.4
 ALL OTHER INDUSTRIES (INCLUDING NOT REPORTED)               32.3
PRIVATE HOUSEHOLD WORKERS                                    19.6
 BABY SITTERS, PRIVATE HOUSEHOLD                             23.2
 HOUSEKEEPERS, PRIVATE HOUSEHOLD                             24.9
 LAUNDRESSES, PRIVATE HOUSEHOLD                              17.6
 PRIVATE HOUSEHOLD WORKERS, NEC                              18.0
```

Appendix C

MEAN, STANDARD DEVIATION, AND PERCENT OF MISSING VALUES FOR MAJOR VARIABLES, BY RACE

Variable	Units	Mean		Standard Deviation		Missing Values (percent)	
		White	Black	White	Black	White	Black
1. Family background							
a. Father's education	ten point scale	2.41	1.66	1.96	1.62	10	22
b. Mother's education	ten point scale	2.79	2.16	1.66	1.50	10	29
c. Father's occupation	prestige score	36.1	28.2	12.3	11.8	0	0
d. Number of siblings		3.64	5.35	2.89	3.95	7	12
2. Number of jobs before entry							
a. Full-time		1.31	.40	2.17	1.26	0	0
b. Part-time		1.13	.47	1.83	1.15	0	0
3. Age at entry	years	18.0	17.3	2.6	2.4	0	0
4. Education	ten point scale						
a. At entry		3.98	3.16	1.77	1.57	0	0
b. Eight years after entry		4.47	3.50	1.89	1.60	0	0
5. Occupational prestige							
a. First job		29.3	24.8	12.0	8.9	1	0
b. One year after entry		30.5	25.5	11.8	8.7	1	1
c. Two years after entry		31.7	26.0	11.4	8.7	0	1
d. Eight years after entry		37.8	27.9	13.8	10.9	0	0
6. Wages*	$1959/month						
a. At start of first job		243	200	136	121	11	13
b. One year after entry		261	214	149	129	9	11
c. Two years after entry		292	226	189	138	8	11
d. Eight years after entry		460	350	260	167	10	7
7. Any military service in the first eight years	dummy variable	.612	.465	.488	.499	0	0

* Percent of additional missing values due to military service:	White	Black
First job	17	16
One year after entry	28	23
Two years after entry	34	28
Eight years after entry	7	9

Variable	1a	1b	1c	1d	2a	2b	3	4a	4b	5a	5b	5c	5d	6a	6b	6c	6d	7
1. Family background																		
a. Father's education	—	.663	.472	-.238	.008	.071	.193	.324	.330	.282	.300	.315	.274	.179	.170	.181	.202	.208
b. Mother's education	.581	—	.342	-.218	.068	.122	.237	.363	.356	.233	.244	.254	.236	.174	.207	.245	.255	.222
c. Father's occupation	.503	.408	—	-.131	.063	.092	.177	.246	.241	.261	.250	.259	.188	.079	.084	.103	.128	.105
d. Number of siblings	-.251	-.306	-.218	—	-.003	-.005	-.100	-.227	-.156	-.114	-.148	-.148	-.131	-.068	-.079	-.114	-.077	-.172
2. Number of jobs before entry																		
a. Full-time	.262	.260	.226	-.210	—	.383	.343	.273	.237	.037	.076	.113	.141	.094	.119	.089	.109	.088
b. Part-time	.096	.162	.152	-.144	.391	—	.241	.232	.230	.014	.025	.074	.063	.080	.124	.090	.095	.144
3. Age at entry	.378	.367	.343	-.279	.608	.399	—	.733	.655	.283	.342	.381	.335	.343	.389	.424	.350	.223
4. Education																		
a. At entry	.421	.395	.366	-.332	.581	.392	.893	—	.945	.357	.420	.466	.481	.351	.410	.449	.409	.346
b. Eight years after entry	.417	.376	.373	-.339	.533	.360	.801	.898	—	.380	.450	.478	.491	.279	.348	.371	.396	.338
5. Occupational prestige																		
a. First job	.211	.248	.230	-.176	.268	.255	.498	.519	.475	—	.859	.748	.411	.215	.241	.258	.194	.134
b. One year after entry	.253	.266	.238	-.185	.331	.325	.537	.565	.519	.762	—	.842	.457	.215	.256	.265	.223	.195
c. Two years after entry	.268	.286	.262	-.180	.325	.314	.549	.576	.524	.671	.825	—	.452	.252	.275	.277	.227	.222
d. Eight years after entry	.257	.294	.274	-.194	.363	.280	.535	.583	.592	.462	.502	.544	—	.129	.173	.185	.267	.218
6. Wages																		
a. At start of first job	.202	.295	.217	-.221	.324	.278	.417	.393	.381	.316	.318	.318	.250	—	.911	.771	.474	.109
b. One year after entry	.212	.280	.237	-.193	.368	.321	.439	.439	.435	.333	.373	.378	.287	.830	—	.881	.529	.127
c. Two years after entry	.128	.212	.165	-.201	.336	.297	.392	.390	.355	.271	.299	.352	.242	.719	.739	—	.528	.108
d. Eight years after entry	.179	.184	.158	-.142	.341	.264	.464	.481	.422	.336	.332	.342	.373	.405	.465	.724	—	.216
7. Any military service in the first eight years	.024	.069	.047	-.088	-.019	-.062	-.024	-.004	.054	-.067	-.130	-.173	-.015	-.030	-.068	-.100	-.061	—

References

Blau, P. M. & O. D. Duncan
1967   *The american occupation structure.* New York: Wiley.
Blum, Z. D.
Validation of retrospective occupational and education experience in life history data. Baltimore: Center for the Study of Social Organization of Schools, Johns Hopkins University.
Blum, Z. D.
1972   White and black careers during the first decade of labor force experience. Part II: Income differences, *Social Science Research* 1, 271–292.
Blum, Z. D., Nancy Karweit, & Aage B. Sorenson
1969   *A method for the collection and analysis of retrospective life histories.* Baltimore: Center for the Study of Social Organization of Schools, Johns Hopkins University.
Bohrnstedt, G. W. & T. M. Carter
1971   Robustness in Regression Analysis. *Sociological methodology 1971,* edited by H. L. Costner. San Francisco: Jossey-Bass. Pp. 118–146.
Bradshaw, T. F.
1973   Jobseeking methods used by unemployed workers, *Monthly Labor Review* 96, 35–40. (Also *Special Labor Force Report* 150).
Browning, H., S. C. Lopreato, & D. L. Preston, Jr.
Income and veteran status, *American Sociological Review* 38, 74–85.
Coleman, J. S., C. C. Berry, & Z. D. Blum
1972   White and black careers during the first decade of labor force experience. Part III: Occupational status and income together, *Social Science Research* 1, 293–304.
Coleman, J. S., Z. D. Blum, A. B. Sørenson, & P. H. Rossi
1972   White and black careers during the first decade of labor force experience. Part I: Occupational status, *Social Science Research* 1, 243–270.
Cooper, S.
1960   Employment of June 1959 high school graduates, October 1959, *Monthly Labor Review* 83, 500–506. (Also *Special Labor Force Report* 5).

Cutright, P.
1974   The civilian earnings of white and black draftees and nonveterans, *American Sociological Review* 39, 317–327.

Davidson, P. E., & H. D. Anderson
1937   *Occupational mobility in an American community.* Palo Alto: Stanford Univ. Press.

Duncan, B.
1967   Education and social background, *American Journal of Sociology* **72**, 363–372.

Duncan, O. D.
1965   The trend of occupational mobility in the United States, *American Sociological Review* 30, 491–498.

Duncan, O. D.
1966   Path analysis: Sociological examples. *American Journal of Sociology* **72**, 1–16.

Duncan, O. D.
1968   Inheritance of poverty on inheritance of Race? In *On understanding poverty*, edited by D. P. Moynihan. New York: Basic Books. Pp. 85–110.

Duncan, O. D., D. L. Featherman, & B. Duncan
1972   *Socioeconomic background and achievement.* New York: Seminar Press.

Duncan, O. D. & R. W. Hodge
1963   Educational and occupational mobility, *American Journal of Sociology* **68**, 629–644.

Featherman, D. L.
1971   A research note: A social structure model for the socioeconomic career, *American Journal of Sociology* **77**, 293–304.

Hamel, H. R.
1966   Employment of high school and dropouts in 1965, *Monthly Labor Review* **89**, 643–649. (Also *Special Labor Force Report* **66**).

Hansen, W. L. & B. A. Weisbrod
1967   Economics of the military draft. *Quarterly Journal of Economics* **81**, 395–421.

Hare, N.
Recent trends in the occupational mobility of negroes, 1930–1960: An intracohort analysis, *Social Forces* **44**, 166–173.

Hayghe, H.
1970   Employment of high school graduates and dropouts, *Monthly Labor Review* **93**, 35–42. (Also *Special Labor Force Report* **121**).

Hayghe, H.
1972   Employment of high school graduates and dropouts, *Monthly Labor Review* **95**, 49–53. (Also *Special Labor Force Report* **145**).

Jencks, C., M. Smith, H. Acland, M. J. Bane, D. Cohen, H. Gintis, B. Heyns, & S. Michelson
1972   *Inequality.* New York: Basic Books.

Kohen, A. & P. Andrisani
1973   *Career thresholds: A longitudinal study of the educational and labor market experience of male youth.* Vol. 4. Columbus, Ohio: The Ohio State Univ. Center for Human Resource Research. Washington, D.C.: U.S. Dept. of Labor, Manpower Administration.

Kohen, A. S. & H. S. Parnes
1971   *Career thresholds: A longitudinal study of the educational and labor market experience of male youth.* Vol. 3. Columbus, Ohio: The Ohio State University Center for Human Resource Research. Washington, D.C.: U.S. Dept. of Labor, Manpower Administration.

Land, K. C.
1969   Principles of path analysis. In *Sociological methodology*, edited by E. F. Borgatta. San Francisco: Jossey-Bass. Pp. 3–37.

Hodge, R. W., P. M. Siegel & P. H. Rossi
1966   Occupational prestige in the United States: 1925–1965. In *Class, status and power,* 2nd ed, edited by R. Bendix and S. M. Lipset. New York: Free Press. Pp. 322–334.

Leiberson, S. & G. V. Fuguitt
1967   Negro-white occupational differences in the absence of discrimination, *American Journal of Sociology* **73**, 188–200.

Lipset, S. M., R. Bendix, & T. Malm
1955   Job plans and entry into the labor market, *Social Forces* **33**, 224–232.

Michelotti, K.
1974   Employment of high school graduates and dropouts, October 1973, *Monthly Labor Review* **97**, 48–52. (Also *Special Labor Force Report* **168**).

Miller, J. C. & R. Tollison
1971   The implicit tax on relevant military recruits, *Social Science Quarterly* **51**, 924–931.

O'Boyle, E. J.
1968   From classroom to workshop: A hazardous journey, *Monthly Labor Review* **91**, 6–12. (Also *Special Labor Force Report* **100**).

Oi, W. Y.
1967   The economic cost of the draft. *American Economic Review* **57**, 39–62.

Parnes, H. S., R. C. Miljus, R. S. Spitz & Associates.
1970   *Career thresholds: A longitudinal study of the educational and labor market experience of male youth.* Vol. 1. Columbus, Ohio: The Ohio State University Center for Human Resource Research. Washington, D.C.: U.S. Dept. of Labor, Manpower Administration.

Perrella, V. C.
1964   Employment of high school graduates and dropouts in 1963, *Monthly Labor Review* **87**, 522–529. (Also *Special Labor Force Report* **41**).

Perrella, V. C.
1969   Employment of high school graduates and dropouts. *Monthly Labor Review* **92**, 36–43. (Also *Special Labor Force Report* **108**).

Piker, J.
   1968   Entry into the labor force; A survey of literature on the experiences of negro and white youths. Ann Arbor, Michigan: Institute of Labor and Industrial Relations.
Porter, J. N.
   1974   Race, socialization and mobility in educational and early occupational attainment, American Sociological Review 39, 303–316.
Reiss, A. J. Jr., O. D. Duncan, P. K. Hatt, & C. C. North
   1961   Occupations and social status, New York: Free Press.
Reynolds, L. G.
   1951   The structure of labor markets, New York: Harper.
Saben, S.
   1967   Occupational mobility of employed workers, Monthly Labor Review 90, 31–38.
Sewell, W. H., A. O. Haller, & G. W. Ohlendorf
   1970   The educational and early occupational status attainment process: Replication and revision, American Sociological Review 35, 1014–1027.
Sewell, W. H., A. O. Haller, & A. Portes
   1969   The educational and early occupational attainment process, American Sociological Review 34, 82–92.
Sheppard, H. L. & A. H. Belitsky
   1966   The job hunt. Baltimore: Johns Hopkins Univ. Press.
Siegel, P. M.
   1965   On the cost of being a negro, Sociological Inquiry 35, 35–47.
Siegel, P. M.
   1970   Prestige in the American occupational structure. Unpublished doctoral dissertation, Univ. of Chicago.
Simpson, R. L. & I. Harper
   1962   Social origins, occupational advice, occupational values and work careers, Social Forces 40, 264–271.
Stigler, G.
   1962   Unemployment and job mobility, Journal of Political Economy 70, 94–106.
U.S. Bureau of the Census
   1970a   Alphabetic index of occupations and industries (1968 Revision). Washington, D.C.: U.S. Government Printing Office.
U.S. Bureau of the Census
   1970b   The statistical abstract of the United States, 90th edition. Washington, D.C.: U.S. Government Printing Office.
U.S. Dept. of Labor, Bureau of Labor Statistics
   1960   School and early employment experience of youth—A report on seven communities, 1952–7. Washington, D.C.: U.S. Government Printing Office.
U.S. Dept. of Labor
   1966   Manpower report of the President. Washington, D.C.: U.S. Government Printing Office.

Young, A. M.
1973 The high school class of 1972: More at work, fewer in college, *Monthly Labor Review* **96**, 26–32. (Also *Special Labor Force Report* **155**.)
Zeller, F. A., J. R. Shea, A. I. Kohen, & J. A. Meyer
1970 *Career thresholds: A longitudinal study of the educational and labor market experience of male youth.* Vol. 2. Columbus, Ohio: The Ohio State University Center for Human Resource Research. Washington, D.C.: U.S. Dept. of Labor, Manpower Administration.

Index

Lieberson, S., 6 n.
Lipset, S. M., 7
Locating Jobs, *see* Methods of locating
    jobs
Lopreato, S. C., 146–147
"Luck," in first job, 5

M

Malm, T., 7
Marital status
    and duration of first job, 123
    at entry into labor force, 52
    and occupational prestige, 64, 155,
        181
    and wages, 68, 94, 158–159
Men, entry of into labor force, 2–3, *see*
        also Entry into labor force
Meyer, J. A., 4
Methods of locating jobs
    classification used, 55
    for first job, 55–56
    and occupation prestige, 64–65,
        92, 155
    and wages 68, 96, 158–159
Michelotti, K., 4 n., 52
Military service
    during the eight years after entry,
        145–149
    first jobs in, 65
    occupational prestige and, 182
    occupational regression and, 157
    second job and, 125
    subsequent careers and, 131
    two years after entry, 87–88, 94
Miljus, R. C., 4
Miller, J. C., 146 n.
Mobility, job, *see* Job mobility
Mother's educational attainment, 28–29
    and full-time jobs before entry, 40
Multivariate analysis in entry process
        studies, 10, *see also* Occupational
        prestige, multivariate analysis;
        Wages, multivariate analysis

N

National Opinion Research Center, 12
Non-blacks, in sample, 16
North, C. C., 17
Number of jobs held, 88–89, 106–109,
        139–145, *see also* Job duration;
        Job mobility

O

O'Boyle, E. J., 4 n., 52, 79
Occupational careers, factors affecting,
        1–3
Occupational experience before entry,
        32–42, *see also* Jobs before entry
Occupational mobility, *see* Job mobility
Occupational prestige
    definition, 16–18
    and duration of first job, 123–125
    educational attainment and, 63–64,
        92, 150–151, 178–179
    eight years after entry, 138
    and family background, 63, 92, 150
    of first job, 45–48, 155
    and geographic moves, 68, 155
    and industry, 65, 92–93, 155–157
    and jobs before entry, 64, 92, 151
    of jobs before entry, 37–39, 41
    and marital status, 64, 155–157
    and method of locating job, 64–65,
        92, 155
    and military service, 65, 156–157
    mobility, 160–163, *see also* Job
        mobility
    multivariate analysis, 61–66, 90–94,
        150–157
    and number of jobs held, 108–117
    one year after entry, 83–85
    racial differences, *see* Blacks
    two years after entry, 83–85, 87
    and wages, 49
Occupational success, main criterion in,
        131–132
Ohlendorf, G. W., 5